Mindful Dog Teaching

Reflections on the Relationships We Share With Our Dogs

- Engagement
- Relationship
- Order
- Stability
- Transcendence

Claudeen E. Mc Auliffe, M. Ed.

Mindful Dog Teaching

For information contact:
Kindness Canine Behavior Consultants LLC
105 West Wisconsin Avenue
Oconomowoc WI 53066
USA
Phone: 262-569-1050
Fax: 262-569-1053
Website: www.kindnessk9.com

ISBN 0-9709367-5-3

Cover Photos by Patricia Arnold-Mora
Cover Design by Patricia Arnold-Mora and Mary Norby

Printed in the U.S.A.

For Kiwi

(Kiwanee)
Awakening
May 22, 2006

For Tom

(Thomas Edison)
Returning
July 24, 2006

Table of Contents

Acknowledgments

This book could not exist without the hundreds of dogs and their humans who enriched and deepened my insights, and without the support of the following mentors, teachers and friends. To all of you, I express deep gratitude:

Dr. Patricia McConnell: Your finest-toothed comb worked the bugs out of the manuscript. You are the standard to which I hold myself.

Linda Tellington-Jones: You opened the door for me into holistic approaches to animal care, as well as to the idea that animal beings are also spiritual beings, and to see the potential for perfection in all beings.

Tom (Thomas Edison): You lit the fire of learning.

Edie Jane Eaton: You gently clarified conceptual issues, provided insights into the Tellington Method, and wrote the Foreword.

Dr. Stanley Coren: Your insights into how dogs think made me think about dogs in a different way.

Suzanne Clothier: You provided lessons in patience.

Stacy Lewis: My friend and colleague, you gave me the jump start I needed to get the manuscript off the computer and into print, and were an honest and critical reviewer.

Mary Norby, Nina Kuper, Polly Cisco, Dr. Kellie Kuzdas, Sue Ann Mc Cotter, Carol Schultz and Pamela Brown-Stace: Your peer reviews showed me things I hadn't thought of.

Mary Norby: My editor and friend, your brilliant ability to see the "big picture" resulted in a more reader-friendly format. Your artistry is reflected in the cover and you crafted the manuscript into its final form as lovingly as if it was your own.

Patricia Arnold-Mora: Your creativity and eye for design dressed the work in an eye-catching and beautiful cover which reflects the words within and your photography captured the spirit within the image.

Foreword

By Edie Jane Eaton

Mindful Teaching! As I read through Claudeen's new book I wondered how much better a rider I would be if I had had a mindful teacher - instead of a military trainer who focused only on what I did wrong, explained nothing, and seemed to delight in reducing his (mostly female) students to tears. He produced some competent Olympic riders, but I wonder at what cost?

Mindful Dog Teaching presents a way of interacting with our dogs which improves our chance of building a solid relationship with them, one that facilitates our teaching and their learning. However, learning is not one-sided and in the ongoing process of our interaction there is an equal amount of them teaching and us learning! Luckily, Claudeen gives suggestions which help us be good students. She also instructs us as playmates: "Play with your dog every day; let him choose the game as often as you do, and let him win some of the time." Fun and fair!

This book has been structured on the basis of E.R.O.S.: Engagement, Relationship, Order and Stability. From order comes stability. We may like a bit of excitement in our lives, but for most of us it is scary when well-known friends behave out of character. Predictability in our companions is usually comforting, and when they have demonstrated reliability and an interest in our well being, we are generally content to do what they ask. We are thankful for such good relationships. Claudeen points out that a relationship develops from an interest in engaging - each with the other. We may be totally engaged by a cute puppy and her endearing ways, but a functional relationship with her will depend upon our demonstrating that we are worth her attention.

We are provided with exercises to help us build relationships and become mindful teachers, with much food for thought mixed with entertaining stories of Claudeen's experiences with many of her own and others' dogs. If you found this book in the "Romance" rather than the "Pet" section of your bookstore or library it may be not only because of it's "EROS"-ic content, but also because it gives fleeting insights into the many loving relationships that Claudeen has had with her dogs while finding her way as she "walks her talk".

As a Tellington TTouch teacher, it delights me to see so many of the principles of the method being applied to more classical techniques of dog training and behaviour management. In her continuing search for a better way to work with animals, Claudeen has explored and studied many disciplines and ideas. I am grateful for her generosity in sharing them with me over the years, and am glad to see some of them presented here.

There are many thoughts to take from this book, but here is one worth keeping in mind always: "See the potential for perfection that may be cloaked in a crooked ear or less than perfect leash manners. Create an environment of cooperation, one dog at a time"

Edie Jane Eaton
Tellington TTouch and TTEAM Instructor
Feldenkrais Practitioner
Alcove, QC
August, 2006

Introduction

Why "Teaching?"

My discipline is the field of education. I am a teacher. I have also been a trainer in the corporate arena. Teaching is different than training. The difference is in the orientation. Teaching focuses on relationship first, task second. Training focuses on task first and relationship second. I teach my students, both dogs and people, to "be" a certain way. I train my students to "do" certain things. Teaching is harder than training because of its relationship aspect, which involves feelings and emotions. Task training often discounts feelings and emotions in favor of achieving certain objectives which are measurable, often in an economic way.

I believe "training" can get in the way of developing appropriate relationships with our animals. The calls I get from people with dog problems often start like this: "My dog needs obedience training." I silently wince when I hear the phrase "obedience training," because it perpetuates the cycle of dominance and submission, and because good training of a dog, or any individual, can't happen without first building a relationship. There is a point in all of our lives, usually when we are young, where we are strongly motivated by the approval of those with whom we have intimate relationships, such as mothers, fathers and grandparents. We are effectively surrogate families for our companion dogs, whose mentation generally is estimated to be that of about a four-year-old human child. If we focus too much on task training with a four-year-old human, social needs will not be met and behavior problems result. I believe dogs are not so different, thus I prefer a teaching orientation to a training one. The mindful teaching of our dogs, with all its rich relationship, is supported by the philosophy described in the chapters to come.

Practicing the New Paradigm

I speak often of paradigms, because they govern our existence, whether or not we are aware of them. In Western culture, a new paradigm is evolving. This paradigm isn't quite evolved enough for many of us to make the shift into it, or perhaps we are not evolved enough to accept it. The paradigm espouses that non-human animals are not lower forms of life, but rather, different forms of life. This is why I feel the concept of hierarchy, especially to the extent that we practice it, gets in the way of our interactions with our dogs and other companion animals. It may be inappropriate to presume to lead or make submissive what constitutes another nation of sentient beings.

Non-Western cultures, such as Native American and Buddhist, traditionally recognize animals and plants as other nations. For Native Americans, the equality of all life is a law of nature. As a human kind of being, the being with the greatest amount of self-determination in the environment we have created on this planet, our responsibility is to provide stewardship for all other kinds of beings. And so any power we feel we have over others instead becomes responsibility toward them. In a 1977 address to the Non-Governmental Organizations of the United Nations in Geneva, Switzerland, Chief Oren Lyons of the Onondaga Nation noted that there were no representatives of the four-footed or winged nations among the assemblage. He stressed the importance of realizing that we are not above the Creation, but are just another part of it, standing "somewhere between the mountain and ant." He reminded us of our responsibility to understand our relationship to all living things, a relationship based on equality rather than superiority.

In fact, many indigenous cultures had no word equivalent to *animal* in their languages. The creatures we call animals were considered by these peoples to be fathers, mothers, sisters, brothers and grandparents. Even in Western cultures, the word *animal* was used mainly by scholars until about the 17th century.

Animal cognition and emotion are provocative fields of study, perhaps creating more questions than answers about the thoughtfulness and feeling with which non-human beings live their lives. If we wish to live well with our animal companions, we necessarily need to consider how their thoughts and feelings impact our relationships.

Western culture is slow to acknowledge that, in addition to thinking and feeling, non-human animals may have spirituality, and a soul as eternal as our own. *Anima*, the Latin root of the word *animal*, means soul or breath of life, and in ancient writings animals and divine forces were often linked. Only in the past twenty years or so have we begun to feel a level of comfort attributing thought and emotion to non-humans. Perhaps we can return to a time when we also attributed to them soul and spirit.

More Than Status

This is not a book about training. It is a book suggesting the type of relationship that needs to be created as a foundation for effective training. Effective training meets several criteria. It is fun for the dog so she learns effortlessly. It is also long lasting: she remembers what she learned because she is a social animal, and her learning is constantly reinforced through social facilitation of a positive nature. Because of its highly social nature, effective training becomes teaching. Mindful Dog Teaching begins with what I believe is a significant barrier to teaching, training, and living well with our dogs: lack of engagement. This lack may result from a general close-mindedness concerning our dogs' abilities to think and reason. It may also be mired in a belief system that dogs, like other animals, are preprogrammed machines devoid of thought and feeling. Or it may come from a place of ignorance, self-interest, laziness or fear. Whatever the roots, lack of engagement limits our ability to take the mindful, proactive approach needed to create a mutually satisfying and enduring relationship.

At one time I believed in the importance of enhancing the status of people who live with dogs, making humans better leaders. I explored this idea in my first book, *Lucy Won't Sit*. With time I began to look more deeply into the nature of relationship with dogs. I asked the question: What is the basis for a successful relationship with a dog? As I considered this question, *Lucy Won't Sit* provoked more questions like "Why won't Lucy sit?" and "Why should Lucy sit?" and, perhaps most importantly, what does "successful relationship" mean? *Lucy* became a threshold beyond which lay answers, thus the first chapter is entitled "Lucy Revisited."

A successful relationship provides for mutual satisfaction of needs which results in the absence of behavior problems. What I learned from Lucy and so many other dogs and their people is that there are two basic things that make successful relationships among social animals possible: respect and cooperation. These two states are less likely to occur when the human is always the leader and the dog is always the follower, and more likely to occur when dogs and humans have equal status, sharing the leadership role depending on the situation. Given the complexity of the dog mind, I find the idea that the human should always be the leader simplistic and limiting. This complexity is becoming clear through recent research on animal cognition and emotion in general, and canine cognition and emotion in particular.

British biologist Rupert Sheldrake argues that our dogs are capable of feats of mind such as telepathy. I do not feel much like a leader in the presence of such company. I do sometimes feel awed and humbled that such a brilliant being as a dog would keep company with me!   In my ten years of working with dogs and their people, I sensed that there had to be something deeper than status driving our interactions with our animals.   I now believe that status is irrelevant to appropriate behavioral outcomes.   Whether you're president, pauper or alpha-bitch, respectful, cooperative behavior is appropriate. Rude, aggressive or overly submissive behavior is not.

Finding Interspecies Synergy

In my practice of teaching dogs, a system of four concepts has emerged and become the philosophy upon which I base my work. I share these here with you. I have found my thoughts crystallizing in the direction of teaching rather than training, direction rather than correction, and facilitation instead of compulsion. I wear the concept of non-human animals being equal to humans like a well-worn shoe. It is comfortable, and comforting.

This book is intended not only to inform, but also to provide a self-help tool. It is a venue of empowerment. *Practice* activities are included to help you pursue involvement and awareness in your relationships with your companion dogs. They are simple but effective over time. It is my wish that in these pages you find empowerment, insights and skills to transcend the boundaries of the human-animal bond, and reach a state of interspecies synergy.

Claudeen E. Mc Auliffe

July 31, 2006

We can do no great things,
only small things with great love.
-- Mother Theresa

Part One

1 Lucy Revisited

*Ahhh . . . Lucy, Lucy, Lucy. She stands in front of the door, gazing at her destination on the other side; a yard full of interesting things. Clearly she has no thought for me, the one standing on my hind legs in front of her, futilely asking for the "sit" which opens the magic door. Might as well try to pluck a star from the sky with my hand. Queen Lucy. High opinion of herself. Doesn't need to play the game. Doesn't need to cooperate. Won't even look my way. "Did I hear you say something?" I see the question in her eyes. Is it my imagination, or did she raise an eyebrow? "Sit, you say? Hah! I don't **DO** sit." The gulf between us is vast.*

Evil Queen Lucy has been sent by her family to board with a professional trainer because she doesn't sit for them either. In fact, she doesn't do a lot of things for them. They, on the other hand, can't do enough for her. She's never satisfied, and her demands have gotten her into trouble since she's started using her teeth to get her way. Ah, Lucy. There must be a better way.

Challenging Our Paradigms

We share with our dogs many endearing characteristics, like generosity, playfulness and self-sacrifice. We also share some that get us into trouble with each other, such as strong emotions, reactivity, the inclination to be opportunistic, and self-interest. Over millennia, humans and dogs have coalesced into an interspecies group. It is the human part of this group that has the greater capacity as well as the responsibility to create order. This is necessarily true because humans are responsible for creating the domesticated world in which domesticated animals like dogs live. From order comes stability. But order isn't possible until a relationship is established, and without engagement there's no relationship. All of this engaging, relating, ordering and stabilizing happens when humans choose to behave in more mindful and proactive ways, rather than mindlessly and reactively. This choice can sometimes be a stretch, due to what I call *habit/expectation paradigms*.

As I counsel clients to help them have better relationships with their dogs, many of my suggestions are met with, "I never thought of that!" If your dog is begging at your table and pulling napkins off your guests' laps, you might try crating your dog with a bone to chew until dinner is over. "I never thought of that!" If your dog sneaks into your child's bedroom to pee, what about closing the door to the bedroom? "I never thought of that!" I smile secretly at this response, because, of course, I was in their shoes once. There were countless times with my first dog when my reply to advice was, "I never thought of that!" Nevertheless I'm amazed at the extent to which we humans allow our dogs to do things that annoy us. It doesn't seem to occur to us that we can prevent a lot of these annoying things by simply changing the environment. This is the effect of well-worn habits and expectations. If the context of an event lies within our experience, habits and expectations, that is to say, within our *habit/expectation paradigm*, the event may pose no problem to manage. But what if the context of the event lies outside our paradigm? The resultant lack of a "fit" creates a disconnect which can make us feel helpless. We are unable to "think out of the box," so to speak, to solve the problem that the non-paradigmatic event now poses.

Habit/expectation paradigms created from our experiences are survival mechanisms which help us cope with overly stimulating and stressful occurrences. But there are many events, such as living with and meeting the needs of another species, that can't fit within our habit/expectation paradigms, and we are often unwilling or unable to confront these events rationally. Life sometimes moves so fast around us that we often think we have no time to really consider a problem in a way that results in a creative and lasting solution. The result is an emotional response of aggression, submission or avoidance.

Interacting with non-human animals can raise our level of consciousness, helping us expand, and even transcend, our habit/expectation paradigms. Non-humans are different from us in so many ways that they necessarily challenge our ways of thinking and acting when we choose to engage them with awareness and mindfulness. Interaction strategies that work with humans don't always work with dogs (making direct eye contact is an example), and so we need to change or expand our habit/expectation paradigms in order to coexist successfully. This involves learning, and learning is also a survival mechanism, a much more expansive, flexible and transformative one than our habit/expectation paradigms. Our dogs have habit/expectation paradigms which, like ours, are shaped by internal and external environmental influences. They also are capable of expanding their paradigms. Like children, however, they usually need our guidance and direction to accomplish this, though there are exceptions. The story of Strongheart, the war dog who became an actor, related by writer J. Allen Boone is an example. With Strongheart's guidance, Boone was able to change his habit/expectation paradigm concerning how animals think and feel. When we and our dogs work together to mutually modify our habit/expectation paradigms, we develop a bond which surpasses mere relationship. Changing a habit or expectation requires a careful choice of approach to set ourselves up for success. The chosen approach may be proactive or reactive.

Proactive or Reactive

What does being proactive or reactive mean? It's the difference between control and crisis. If we can anticipate something will happen, we can create a step-by-step plan to manage it so it has a better chance of a successful and predictable outcome. That's being proactive and responsible. If we don't have a plan, whatever happens just kind of carries us along with it, and whatever right we may have thought we had to good behavior from our dog gets subrogated to our lack of planning and responsibility. The event becomes a crisis. This is a reactive state, and crisis management is stressful. If I know, for example, that my dog generally ignores my call to come, a proactive approach is to always use a leash so I can guide the dog in my direction, insuring a successful and predictable outcome. If I refuse to use a leash on such a dog, she may run away and have a high probability of being stolen, poisoned, or run over, a crisis to which I will probably react emotionally rather than rationally. Such incidents have the cumulative effect of not only damaging an already-compromised relationship, but also of causing us to think that dogs do calculated and deliberate things to make our lives miserable, which, of course, they usually don't. They just do what works. By taking a proactive approach, we anticipate the dog's response to a given situation, and we understand that because of our ability to think more logically than the dog, it's our responsibility to guide her toward behaviors that work as well for us as they do for her.

Proactive and reactive approaches affect the relationship between humans and dogs. Proactive and reactive approaches to a situation have two attributes in common: what we pay attention to, and what we feel. The combination of attention and feeling generates a certain outcome. We can influence outcomes by changing what we pay attention to and how we feel about what we are observing. Figure 1 shows reactive and proactive approaches to two common dog misbehaviors, destructive chewing and running away. Note the behaviors generated by the feelings in each approach. Which approach is the more organized and useful?

Becoming proactive is difficult without engagement. Just as we mindfully turn a radio dial to tune in to the frequency that provides the greatest clarity, we mindfully tune in to the individual with whom we're trying to solve a problem, meet a challenge, or build a relationship. I call this tuning in "engagement." It provides the clarity needed to resolve issues, and it works as well with dogs as it does with humans.

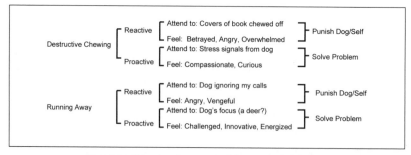

Figure 1. Proactive and reactive approaches to two common dog behaviors.

Curiously, sometimes the more we ignore them, the more dogs seek to engage us. And the more we cater to them, the less dogs seek to engage us, as Lucy demonstrates by her refusal to sit. The key is to strike a balance. By ordering the elements of relationship, balance is achieved and the relationship acquires the stability needed to endure. The proactive approach is a tool to this end.

Adapting, Choosing and Changing

*Lucy doesn't seem to see a lot of value in sitting; after all, no one at home ever asks her to do it. They just give her what she wants. Doesn't she have them **that** well-trained! But here . . . Here is a crossroads. You're not at home anymore, Lucy. What you did there doesn't work here. Might you consider changing what you do, so it works here? How can I help you make the right choice, so that what you do works to get you what you want in this new place?*

Emotions motivate behavior. Behavior changes when emotional state changes. The power to change an emotional state lies within the individual experiencing that emotion. Whether or not we are aware of it, we always have choices about what we feel and what we do in response to any situation. Thus I cannot change another's emotions or behavior. The power does not reside with me. But I do have the power to change the environment around the individual in ways that cause her to create, within the limits of her capacity, different emotions and behaviors. And she makes those changes, often with little resistance, because those are what work in the different environment to more easily get her what she wants.

Each of us is different in our emotional and behavioral responses to situations. A mindful and proactive approach will take into account these differences, allowing them to guide the practice of teaching. With mindfulness, and by being proactive, I can change my own emotions and behavior, managing the environment so that the other individual reacts to my changes in a way that satisfies our respective needs. Based on this, my strategy for working with people and dogs who have issues is this: change the environment within and around the dog, and the dog will adapt its behaviors to the new environment. In practice it might look something like the following:

> I step out of the room to get a cup of coffee, leaving my new pup unsupervised. I return three minutes later to find a shredded book in the middle of the floor. But what if, before I step out for that second cup of coffee, I put pup in the crate with a bone. No shredded books or other surprises!

I work with the things I can control, then call on the adaptive capacity of the dog to change in response to the new environment I've created. Book shredding will likely disappear with puppy teeth, provided I create an environment in which pup doesn't get a chance to practice book shredding in favor of more constructive pursuits like bone chewing. I haven't done any training, but I've set my dog up for success by proactively changing my own response to a problem.

To change a certain emotional state – fear, for example, which is motivating the behavior of running away whenever the nail clippers appear – I set the clippers at a distance where the dog displays calmness, feeding bits of steak each time the dog looks at the item. I gradually move the clippers closer, until the dog learns to accept the actual sensation of nail cutting, mindful to maintain the calm state by never exceeding the dog's threshold for change. Thus I have created conditions in the environment which allow the dog to think and make appropriate choices.

> *We are both waiting. I haven't changed my expectation that Lucy sits before going outside. Instead of coercing, I change my attitude and behavior. I engage her by taking a small step in her direction, causing her to look up at me. I again ask Lucy to sit. This time her posterior drops immediately to the floor as she gives me eye contact. By this time she's probably tired of standing.*

Playing the waiting game paid off, which is to say, once you engage, you dare not stop until you reach your goal, or your dog will never take you seriously. Persistence also is part of the new environment. The best animal trainers get that way because they take as much time as they need to capture exactly the behavior they want to reinforce.

I open the door, releasing Lucy to the great outdoors. Changing my behavior (repositioning my body, controlling my frustration, and being patient) changed the environment, and Lucy reacted with a cooperative response.

Why Does Lucy Need to Sit?

Lucy's willingness to sit met my need for cooperation and respect, and by continuing such exchanges we can begin to build a relationship that will help achieve the goals her family has set for her behavior. More significantly, the act of sitting in exchange for access to something the dog values is symbolic of the reciprocal nature of the union between dogs and humans. This simple expression of "give-and-take" is a hallmark of right communal living.

Social animals form communities to meet individual and group needs through cooperation. Harmonious coexistence is usually desirable. This is achieved by behaving in ways that acknowledge and respect each others' rights and responsibilities. The rights of one become the responsibilities of the other, and the reverse is also true. What are the rights and responsibilities when one member of the community is a human, and the other is a dog?

Dogs have teeth and claws. Used in the wrong way, these may represent an unacceptable level of risk to the community. The members of the community have the right to safety, one of the reasons the community probably formed in the first place. So one of my responsibilities to Lucy is to prevent her from ever using her armament in destructive ways, something she has a history of doing, which is why she has come under my care. As a member of the community, I have the right to safety, which is why muscling Lucy into a sit by pushing on her posterior is probably not in my best interest. So I also have the responsibility to think through my plan to get Lucy to sit, making sure I won't make her antagonistic attitude worse. Rather than demanding and taking what they want at the expense of other community members, respectful individuals exchange items of like value. That way everyone wins. Winning makes us feel good and reinforces cooperation because we got something we wanted in exchange for working together. Sitting is an expression of cooperation.

And so, dear Lucy, can you even imagine the possibilities? If only you will sit, all the world is your personal prime rib! You might even get to swim in the pond!

****

Reflections . . .

1. Habit/expectation paradigms are survival mechanisms.
2. Interacting with non-human animals helps expand our habit/expectation paradigms.
3. A proactive approach anticipates while a reactive approach copes.
4. Observations, feelings and approaches create outcomes.
5. We can't change another's feelings or behavior.

6. We *can* mindfully and proactively change our feelings and behavior.
7. Communities consist of individuals with rights and responsibilities toward each other.
8. Respect prompts reciprocity and everyone wins.

The difference between us is one of degree, not kind.

— Roger Fouts

2 Engagement

engagement \in-'gāj-mənt\ 4: to come together and interlock.

facilitated by: communication

Getting Things Moving

We make a commitment to our canine companion, and we usually intend it to last a lifetime. This commitment blossoms fully when we're engaged with our animals. We've made a connection, often on a deeply emotional and spiritual level. When such a connection is made, our perspective toward the other changes. I believe this is true for us as well as our dogs. Engagement with another means we're more tolerant of mistakes, more patient with misunderstandings, quick to forgive, and always believing that our partner is fundamentally good and well-meaning towards us. As a behavior consultant, my biggest concern is helping my clients understand the importance of creating engagement with their dogs, because without engagement no treatment plan can be completely successful.

Engagement means to put things into motion. "Trekkies" will recall Captain Jean-Luc Picard's "Engage!" command which put the Enterprise into motion toward resolving another galactic dilemma. When the officers on the bridge of Enterprise see a strange ship, they try to communicate with it. Communication, including touching, talking, listening, smelling and tasting, gets things moving. It creates engagement. Here's where we can take a lesson from our dogs: they constantly communicate with and engage their environment. Watch a dog for ten minutes and count the number of times she sniffs, tastes, listens, touches or woofs in response to some environmental cue.   To a dog, being awake is synonymous with being engaged, and engagement is life itself!   In an optimal environment, life never passes a dog by.   She lives it fully, engaging with it every second.   This same level of involvement is what we must practice with our dogs if we wish to have a satisfying and problem-free relationship with them.

Attraction

When "Engage!" is heard on the bridge of the Enterprise, it's because there's something out there in the universe exerting a force that attracts Enterprise in its direction.   Attraction goes beyond mere interest, drawing us toward something.   It is a form of communication which nature implements in obvious and subtle ways to create engagement.

The attractive sight of a deer, for example, initiates a chase. The attractive sound of my husband's tread on the porch initiates dogs rushing to the door.   The attractive feel of my touch makes Tom the dog snuggle closer.   The attractive taste of pasta causes me to eat more than I should.   The attractive smell of a rabbit draws a beagle's nose to the ground.   Subtler attractive influences include hormones, pheromones, telepathy and morphogenetic fields.   Some are measurable, some are not.   However, our inability to measure some of these phenomena does not invalidate them or diminish their influence.

NO . . . NO . . . NO

It is regrettable that our efforts to communicate with our dogs sometimes create disengagement by being repellant rather than attractive.   Our verbal communication often consists of confusingly large numbers of words with many hidden assumptions.   Take, for example, the apparently simple word *no*. *No* is the opposite of *yes.* It communicates the perception of a disorderly state of affairs.   Underlying the word *no* are the following assumptions:
- Whatever *no* refers to is inappropriate.
- One should stop doing activities that result in the expression of *no.*

- When one hears *no*, that individual understands they have done an inappropriate thing.

There are probably other assumptions, but let's look at just these three from a dog's perspective.

*Whatever **no** refers to is inappropriate.* Dogs may eventually make the connection between their inappropriate action, the expression of *no*, and the displeasure of the one sending the *no* message. Part of this eventual understanding may be due to the genetics of the dog, or it may be the result of simple repetition over time. But repetition of mistakes over time and without learning is tedious. The trial and error learning which this repetition involves is inefficient, frustrating, and can erode self-esteem, even in the strongest of individuals. In the process of trying to work out the connections between their actions and their humans' displeasure, sensitive individuals may shut down. More stalwart ones may use aggressive tactics. Neither approach promotes engagement and both may generate a lot of resistance.

An example of "shutting down" is demonstrated in dogs who roll onto their backs in response to being asked to do something like accept the leash being attached to the collar. When hands are placed on or around the dog's body to lift him back onto his feet, he may rabbit kick vigorously. If rabbit kicking is unsuccessful, mouthing or biting may be the next step. Rolling onto the back in response to a challenge is a display of submission in some dogs, especially when it's accompanied by an exposed throat, licking of the lips, and averted eyes. But when it's accompanied by direct eye contact, it may indicate the dog's desire to confront what it cannot escape from, and she can be more than a match for grasping hands by biting and kicking with four clawed feet.

*One should stop doing activities that result in the expression of **no**.* This is an implied (by the sender of no) assumption that most dogs and very young children don't mentally grasp because of their developmental state, and possibly because of the mixed message described in the next paragraph.

*When one hears **no**, that individual understands they have done an inappropriate thing.* This assumption implies that the sender of **no** and receiver of **no** have the same values, and will thus have the same understanding about what is appropriate or inappropriate. Dogs and humans often have conflicting values, and what dogs consider appropriate is often considered the opposite by humans; marking territory in the house, for example.

This assumption may also pose a conflict because what we imply the word *no* to mean is contradicted by the way we express it. The vocalization of "No" inadvertently provides attention, thus reinforcing the inappropriate behavior. This reinforcing effect is increased by direct eye contact and some movement or orientation in the dog's direction, which often accompanies the word. Because our intent and our actions are not in agreement, the attention, though of low quality, reinforces the inappropriate behavior, so it will likely happen again.

To clarify the miscommunication and decrease the disengagement implicit in the word *no*, I ask my clients if they would be willing to do a role play with me to understand better why the word *no* may unhelpful. I explain that the word *no* conveys limited information to the dog, and that it's important to tell our dog specifically what we expect, minus any implicit assumptions that may be confusing. I then have in mind, but don't disclose to the client, changing something the client is doing, for example, holding the leash too tightly. Following is an example of the role play dialogue:

Me: *[direct eye contact, relaxed face, leaning slightly toward client]* "No."

Client: *Does nothing; may look at me politely and expectantly.*

Me: *[direct eye contact, leaning toward client, somewhat tighter face, louder]* "NO."

Client: *Does nothing; may fidget, shift eyes; begins to look uncomfortable; tightens grip on leash.*
(Note that my emotional state gets the opposite effect of what I want.)

Me:	*[harder eye contact, louder voice]* "I said NO!"
Client:	*Looks very uncomfortable; may apologize for not knowing what I want.*
Me:	*[neutral, conversational tone, softer eye contact]* "Slack your leash."
Client:	*Allows some slack in leash.*
Me:	*[neutral, conversational tone, softer eye contact]* "Good."
Client:	*Posture relaxes, face looks relieved.*
Me:	*[soft eye contact, helpful tone]* "Slack your leash a little more."
Client:	*Allows more slack.*
Me:	*[smiling, happy voice]* "Good!"
Client:	*Smiling.*

As we process this experience, especially the emotions embedded in the words and facial expressions, most clients begin to understand the importance of directing appropriate behaviors by clearly expressing their needs, rather than correcting inappropriate behaviors with mixed messages of reinforcement masked by overt disapproval.[1] During one of these role plays, I was working with a nine-year-old girl and her mother. In our discussion after the exercise, I commented that the number of overcrowded correctional institutions attests to the power of negative language in our culture, and that we would probably need far fewer of these repositories of inappropriate behavior if we learned to clearly express our needs. At this point the girl looked at me and said brightly, "Maybe we should call them 'directional' institutions!" I love working with nine-year-olds; they get it!

Beyond No

In addition to our verbal communication, our body language can also be repellent. We often see dogs unwilling to approach humans who are directly facing them, but dogs often come quickly when we begin to move away from them

---

[1] The concept of direction replacing correction originated from the synergy of the Tellington Method practitioners.

with our body turned sideways. Dogs also know when we're smiling and when we're not, and are able to interpret our facial expressions. A happy disposition reflected in a smiling face, or a sad one in a frown, also creates chemical shifts in the body which may cause us to smell a certain way, hence expressions like "the smell of fear." Our chemical state, and thus our smell, may be attractive or repulsive to our dogs.

Dogs may be repelled by the sounds humans make. A pervasive myth is that women don't make good trainers because their voices are too high-pitched. In actuality, dogs are drawn more to high-pitched voices than they are to low, growly ones.

Touch can be repellent. A dog that is struck even once may learn to shrink from hands coming in his direction. I watched an elderly gentleman interact with his pointer. I'm sure he was fond of his dog; however, he demonstrated this by audibly whacking the dog with the flat of his hand over its back and shoulders. In response the dog hung her head with her ears well back, whites of eyes showing.

Some dogs are aversive to touch irrespective of bad experiences with it. This is true of humans as well, with some of us being more "touchy-feely" than others. Forcing an animal, non-human or otherwise to accept touching, disrespects that individual. Dogs may suffer our hugs, preferring to interact in other ways. Discovering their preferred ways of interacting is critical to creating engagement with these individuals, and may require patience and creativity.

A Dog's Choice

Engagement with our dogs should be easy. After all, attending to and engaging with humans is one of the things that made domestication of the dog possible. Our dogs appear to have a genetic predisposition to engage with us, even treating us as they do others of their species.

I fostered Glory for several weeks. Returned to the shelter from an adoptive home, he was said to be destructive. When I picked him up, he was struggling with an upper respiratory infection and was horribly dirty, smelling of urine, and oozing pus from sores on his elbows. I gingerly loaded him in the back of my car, tethering him with a harness and coupler to contain him and prevent any efforts to help me drive. On my arrival home, my intent was to leave him tethered in the car for a few minutes while I went up to the house to secure my dogs. The car windows were open halfway, not enough, I thought, for this skinny, 50-pound Lab mix to escape. I ran to the house, secured dogs, turned to open the door to get him from the car, and voilá! There he was on the porch! Remnants of chewed tether dangled from his harness. He sat there looking at me with tulip ears pricked and head cocked, as if to say, "What's next?"

Glory and I had just met. No relationship existed. He could have been miles down the road in pursuit of his own singular interests. He had chosen instead to seek me out. Maybe he realized it was I who had gotten him out of jail. We'll never know. This is engagement! Of course I reciprocated, welcoming him in the front door. The next stop was the bathtub!

To engage with our dogs is to more fully engage with ourselves, others and our world. In this age of disengagement, where we can easily live our lives without direct contact with anyone, this is a very significant thing, indeed!

A Balanced Approach

Our approach to a situation, combined with our mindset, may promote or discourage engagement. Mindful practices, whether proactive or reactive tend to promote engagement; mindless practices tend to promote disengagement. Achieving balance between proactive and reactive approaches can be challenging.

Figure 3 illustrates possible combinations of approaches and mindsets, their characteristics, and potential results. Figure 4 gives an example of each approach/mindset combination as it might relate to dealing with a dog who has a tendency to run away.

		APPROACH	
		Proactive	Reactive
MINDSET	Mindful	Characteristics: • Deliberate • Predictable results • Adaptive to change Result: • Expand habit/expectation paradigms	Characteristics: • Eclectic • Creative • Serendipitous Result: • Transform habit/expectation paradigms
	Mindless	Characteristics: • Action without thought • Non-adaptive to change • Unpredictable results • Crisis producing Result: • Reinforce narrow habit/expectation paradigms	Characteristics: • Knee-jerk • Reflexive • Chaotic Result: • Reinforce narrow habit/expectation paradigms • Fight/flight response

Figure 3. Approach-Mindset Characteristics and Potential Effects

A proactive approach builds engagement by anticipating outcomes. A reactive approach copes with events as they happen. When a reactive approach is mindful, it may promote engagement through the sharing of a positive but unforeseen outcome. A mindless, proactive approach may promote disengagement, because it may focus on an outcome irrespective of relationship dynamics. A reactive, mindless approach increases the likelihood of disengagement;

outcomes are determined by external forces. Such outcomes, which may result from chronic stress, are often not what we would choose for ourselves or others if we really thought about it.

		APPROACH	
		Proactive	Reactive
MINDSET	Mindful	• Lure approach with food or chase game. • When she catches you, reward with something dog values. • Approach for reward becomes habitual.	• Car suddenly coming toward us on the road. • I run into a field. • Dog chases me; we are out of danger. • We discover a trail not visible from the road. • Approach becomes more likely due to element of happy surprise.
	Mindless	• Long line on dog. • Reel him in when he ignores recall cue. • Resistance and avoidance may become habitual, especially for sensitive dogs.	• Beat the dog for a tardy recall. • Avoidance becomes habitual due to fear of pain.

Figure 4. Examples of Different Approach-Mindset Combinations

Increasing awareness of our habit/expectation paradigms through mindfulness allows us to expand or change them using proactive and reactive approaches to situations. Moshe Feldenkrais, an Israeli physicist, whose Feldenkrais method of bodywork helped inspire the development of the Tellington Method®, said, "When you know what you do, you can do what you want." When we take time to become aware of what we do, and learn how we do it, we increase the probability that our reactions will be mindful rather than mindless. The number of options available to us in any given situation is increased.

Caveat

Some dogs find no value in engaging with humans. They prefer the company of other dogs, or may even wish to be solitary. This is more about temperament than about our failure to find a way into these dogs' hearts or minds. Solitary dogs can be a great source of frustration to clients who anticipate and even embrace a degree of dependency from their dogs. Having dependents whose needs we adequately meet is a great source of pride and accomplishment. For many who have lost other connections, caring for a companion animal provides the motivation to live from one day to the next.

Dogs with solitary inclinations are often loved no less than social ones. Despite their aloofness, they do have needs for other things such as food, exercise, safety, possible interaction with other dogs, and perhaps a job that allows for the expression of their unique abilities. A mindful approach to meeting the needs of such a dog may create perspective on this challenge, and acceptance of it. It may become an altruistic pursuit from which one expects no reciprocity except the knowledge and satisfaction that the needs of another individual were adequately provided for. If we cannot engage with the individual, engagement with the process may be enough. Engagement, whatever form it takes, is fundamental to creating and maintaining relationship.

****

Reflections . . .

1. Engagement is fundamental to creating and maintaining relationship.
2. Attraction is a form of communication which facilitates engagement.
3. Some efforts to communicate may repel rather than attract.
4. It appears that our dogs are genetically programmed to engage with us.
5. Engagement results from approach in combination with mindset.
6. Mindfulness can help determine the right approach.
7. Some dogs find no value in engaging with humans.

Proceed eclectically and creatively.

— Stanislav Grof

3   Relationship

relationship   \ri-'lā-shən-,ship\   3b. a romantic or passionate attachment.

facilitated by: need

Why Relate?

We create relationships to satisfy needs and desires. If there is no need or desire, there is no functional relationship. We often don't seem to pay attention to our dogs in ways that satisfy their needs and desires. We may even take our dogs and their needs/desires for granted. When needs are not satisfied, and the fulfillment of desires is frustrated, behavior issues result. Problem behaviors, in many cases, are attempts to get needs met.

Creating engagement and developing relationship with our dogs necessitates giving from our substance and not of our surplus. When we arrive home very tired at the end of a workday, perhaps we don't take time to accommodate the needs of a dog who has been waiting all day for our return. This is selfish. If we don't have time to meet our dogs' needs, why do we have dogs?

Snowball the Samoyed spent his day tethered in the tiny backyard. Arnie, his human, was in the midst of a divorce and worked two jobs to make ends meet. Arnie left for work at 6 am, often not returning till late in the evening. Arnie's girlfriend stopped by to make sure Snowball had

food and water, and wasn't tangled in his tether. Snowball was digging holes in the yard and chewing a hole in the fence.

On nights when Arnie wasn't too tired, he would lie on the couch and watch TV. Snowball kept him company, but Snowball's pacing and whining annoyed Arnie. I commented that Snowball's needs for exercise and social stimulation were not being met, and this could be causing the behavior problems. I asked Arnie why, with his demanding life, he had a dog. His response, "When I'm laying there on the couch, and he comes up and licks my face, awww, I just love that." "So," I said, "Snowball is meeting your needs, but who is meeting Snowball's needs?"

Biologists Raymond and Lorna Coppinger describe several different possible relationships that dogs and a few other species can have with humans, indicating that relationships between us are not at all clear, and differ among cultural contexts. Most of us probably subscribe to the belief that the relationship we share with our dogs is one of *mutualism*, where both species' needs are satisfied in usually positive ways from their interactions. But other types of relationships are possible, including *commensalism*, where the needs of only one species are met. Scavengers, for example, get food from village dumps but do not interact with the villagers themselves. Another type of relationship is *parasitism*, where one species satisfies its needs at the expense of another. A recent client illustrates this type of relationship, where the dog was so badly behaved and created so much liability that one family member needed to see a therapist and began taking antidepressant drugs. *Amensalism* is yet a fourth type of relationship where one species harms the other out of ignorance and receives no benefit in the process. The Coppingers provide the example of purebred dogs whose increasingly concentrated gene pools may ultimately result in their demise.

How might these different types of relationships affect the ways in which we meet our dogs' needs? Clearly the needs of a parasite, in most cases, would not be taken as seriously as the needs of one with whom we engage in a mutualistic type of relationship. Perhaps in deciding to form a relationship with our dogs, we need to quite seriously consider what type of relationship we will pursue. We also may need to ask ourselves, "What is the current state of relationship?" and, perhaps more importantly, "Do we want to change it?"

That all things created are related is a governing principle of many indigenous cultures, such as Australian Aborigines and Native American Indians. These peoples practice a high level of mutualism across species. Creating and maintaining mutualistic relationships is resource-intensive and full of uncertainty, including the unexpected or misunderstood emotions and behaviors of those with whom we are attempting to relate. Perhaps it is because mutualism is demanding that we have devised technological ways of meeting needs. Technology does not leave so much to chance and is so much more predictable and controllable. Thus it is safer. Safety is good.

The capacity of our habit/expectation paradigm for flexibility and transformation diminishes as we become a technological race. Flexibility and transformation are risky and unsafe. One of my college professors continually reminded us that unchanging misery is preferred to the misery of change. If we choose, we can live our entire adult lives without having to relate much to others. Because of computers and the Internet, for example, there are few products and services that can't be provided remotely, and this is not always to our advantage. I find online access to rescue dogs, for example, disturbing. Local candidates for adoption may be passed over. There is also little opportunity for pre-adoption interaction with online candidates, which may place us immediately into a state of crisis management when they arrive in our home carrying baggage we couldn't anticipate.

Not so terribly long ago, satisfaction of many needs and desires depended on cultivating relationship. My mother was more likely to get good cuts of meat from the butcher if she spent a few minutes chatting with him. Face-to-face communication is the glue which holds relationships together. It helps us express our needs in a spontaneous dialogue enriched with facial expressions, eye contact, body language, and undistorted voices.

Our hunter-gatherer ancestors survived by engaging and cultivating relationships with animals, plants, weather, and many other aspects of nature. Paying close attention to the natural world was synonymous with survival. Humans were comparatively fragile beings and may have gained a survival advantage by using the perceptions of non-human beings to compensate for their shortcomings, relying, for example, on the more acute senses of the proto-dogs at the camp fringe to warn them of approaching predators or strangers.

How does the satisfaction of need and fulfillment of desire pertain to the development of relationship between us and our dogs? In my work I find many relationships, such as the one Arnie and Snowball shared, that are not mutualistic. Most humans seem unaware that the needs of another species may be different from their own, or that they have needs at all. A dog satisfies a human's need for a warm, fuzzy, dependent. Many of us humans like the idea of perpetual dependents. It makes us feel needed, which give us a sense of self-worth. Dogs by their very nature are experts at making us feel needed. But there may be little or no reciprocity, and this forced dependency actually represents a type of enslavement where the dog's need for engagement, activity, direction, a job, achievement and even self-actualization go unmet. Thus we have a behavior problem.

So why relate? Not only to resolve behavior issues, but to prevent them. It may take less effort to build a healthy relationship than it does to resolve the issues that result from an unhealthy relationship.

About Power and Control

When I meet a dog for the first time, I try to respect the animal's need for psychological as well as physical safety. I'm mindful of my body language, avoid direct eye contact, and stay out of the animal's space. This is a lot like warming the butter to room temperature before trying to blend it with the sugar in your favorite chocolate chip cookie recipe; you get less resistance and a smoother result.

This is not to say that I allow the dog to do anything she pleases, and I do assert myself if a dog's behavior is too forward. But what I try to achieve is balance between us where neither is striving for power and control over the other. Instead, I focus on developing the power of relationship, where power and control transmute into respect and influence. The realization of this simple (or perhaps not!) transmutation sent my work with clients light years forward. It felt freeing, no longer needing to focus on who's in charge, who's not, or who's trying to be.

Where there's a struggle for power and control, there's a lack of respect and self-confidence that creates fear in those who are attempting to participate in relationship. This fear makes power and control necessary. Ignorance creates fear. My strategy has been to educate my clients, empower them with knowledge, and develop competence. This helps replace their fear with courage, confidence and hope, helping them realize that they have considerable influence over their dog's behaviors if only they have the respect for self and other that supports their influence.

Lesson of the Monster Puppy

"One of our clients is going into the hospital for an extended period. He'll be in treatment for six months. We can't keep his dog that long. Would you be interested in boarding Tessie and doing some training?" So went the call from a local kennel. "Sure," I said, clueless to the chaos in my future. Runaway locomotive/chain saw/paper shredder/tornado alert siren – Tessie, the monster puppy: challenge and teacher.

The first night she destroyed her bed, howled non-stop till about three in the morning, greeted the sunrise with more howling, inhaled her breakfast, then exhaled at least three times its volume the length and breadth of her freshly cleaned kennel. At eleven months she knew nothing of sit, down, stay or come. Her greatest pleasure was swimming obsessive circles in the pond, which she would do to exhaustion if we let her. She would look at my face, but from her expression I had to conclude I was invisible and she was fixated with wide eyes on something behind my head. She seemed unreachable.

Her lack of focus exasperated me. Her destructiveness angered me. The most dreadful unkindnesses crossed my lips concerning her owner's inattention to his dog's social skills. I was inclined to be neither compassionate nor sensitive. I didn't care that I might jerk too hard on her collar when she repeatedly tried to run away. I kept telling myself she was irredeemable and bent on making my life a misery. Though the realization didn't occur till sometime later, I was transferring onto Tessie the dislike I felt for her owner – a spoiled, immature middle-aged man who knew nothing about caring for himself much less raising a dog.

In such cases it's important to stop thinking the unproductive, self-defeating thoughts that take control of us when we're in stressful situations. This is reactive. Instead, though it's not easy, choose to think positive, coping thoughts.

One afternoon I sat down in front of Tessie's kennel, while she leapt wildly up against the fence. I sat silently for some time, watching her. Finally the leaping became pacing. She sat down and looked at me with an expression that seemed to say, "I see you. What!" I took a deep breath. I began to speak to her quietly as I looked into her eyes. "Tessie, you're being a jerk. You make me mad. I know you can't help yourself, but I'm fed up with your behavior. If you weren't

> *somebody else's dog, I'd drop kick you over the river. You need to work with me, Tessie."*
>
> *We looked at each other through the fence for a few more minutes, during which time she laid down and put her nose on her paws. I told her what a good girl she was for being quiet. I took a deep breath.*

Regardless of the peculiarities of Tessie's owner, I had to ask myself how much I may have gotten in the way of progress by transferring my dislike of the person to his dog. When I admitted this and accepted responsibility for it, I was able to change my attitude toward Tessie. Her behavior was absolutely not her fault. On this basis we started to engage and relate. As we both relaxed, teaching began in earnest. I could hardly believe it when one morning I opened her kennel door, and she actually waited to be invited out.

So what was the lesson of the monster puppy? It was that mindless, reactive behaviors are contagious and powerfully influence relationships in negative ways. It was also that those not directly involved in a relationship we're trying to build may be influential without our knowledge. Before we reach the point of desperation, we may want to just sit down in front of our nemesis and take a few deep breaths together. The real nemesis may be us!

She's My Baby . . . I Love Her to Death!

Tessie's owner really did love her almost to death, calling her "my queen" and indulging her to the point where both of them were behaving obnoxiously. She was so out of control she chewed her way into his kitchen cabinet for a nearly lethal snack of rat poison. I wish I had a dollar for every time a potential client calling for an appointment says to me, "She's my baby . . . I love her to death!"   I think to myself, "Well, you may get your wish if things continue on their present course." We're trying to build a relationship with another species who has different values and beliefs.   Not only is it incredibly disrespectful to treat a dog, or any other species for that matter, like a human infant, but if you love your dog to death, she may just be out of control enough to warrant a death sentence, self-inflicted or otherwise. Most of the time "She's my baby" means, "I set no limits, I have no boundaries or expectations, I am unable or unwilling to articulate my needs in my relationship with you," and I often hear it in conjunction with dogs who have been adopted from rescues or shelters.

These are animals who have not always had the best things happen to them in their lives, and we're going to make it up to them. So we try to make their lives as easy, undemanding and carefree as we can, in reparation for all they've suffered. This well-meaning but naïve approach almost never fails to create problems, as the dog, far from feeling relieved upon its arrival at heaven on earth, becomes totally ungrounded due to the lack of structure. She drifts from one trial and error experience to another, attempting to make sense of the unpredictable environment.

Marie and her son Allen were allergic to dogs, but they wanted one anyway. So they adopted a Lhasa/Shih-tzu mix from a rescue. All they knew of the dog's history was that she had been surrendered by a man who had received her as a gift from his girlfriend. He had moved to an apartment and couldn't take his dog with him. From experience I knew there was probably more to the story.

The dog, Racer, was perfect in every way except one. She was making a toilet of Marie's house. I reviewed remedial housetraining with Marie and Allen while I observed the dog. She seemed unusually unspirited for a four-year-old. This was the family's first dog. In the process of our conversation, it became abundantly clear that while Racer was meeting most of Marie and Allen's needs, they weren't reciprocating in a way that Racer found very useful. I asked Allen about the status of Racer's response to cues such as sit, down and come. "She doesn't do any of those things," he confessed. With a piece of freeze-dried liver I got Racer

to do half a dozen respectable sits and recalls. I saw more engagement from her in this 30 seconds than I had in the entire 90 minute consultation. Racer's eyes were bright as she worked with me. Allen's mouth fell open as he watched, unable to believe what he was seeing. Toward the end of the session, I looked at Marie and said, "You know, you have a brilliant dog here. The problem is that you have no expectations of her, whatsoever. The housesoiling isn't the problem. It's your lack of engagement that's driving this issue." I'm not usually this blunt with my clients, but I took a calculated risk that Marie and Allen were open-minded enough to trust me, based on their positive response to some of the other recommendations I'd made. They agreed to take Racer to a clicker training class to become more engaged with their dog. I think my calculated risk paid off. When they left, Allen was able to get Racer to sit before he opened the door. As they walked away I overheard him say to Marie, "That was fun! We should have done this before!"

How empowering a little structure can be!

Don't Bite the Dog

It seems to me that when force is used, the interaction ceases to be about the dog, and is more concerned with our feelings about ourselves. When we honestly like and accept ourselves, and admit that we are a work in progress, we are more likely to accept others. We forego the posturing intended to create an impression that may reflect something other than who or what we are. Such posturing can be emotionally charged.

While emotionally-charged posturing may be part of the "human condition," its effect on relationship is to provoke avoidance rather than approach. Bullies tend to be unpopular except within their own counterculture. So as we work to develop a mutually respectful relationship with our dogs, we need to manage or discard any of our behaviors which cause our dogs to be fearful. This includes angry, aggressive, reactive outbursts. To avoid or extinguish these behaviors, we first need to become aware of them, and appreciate the harm they do to our relationships.   Fear-producing behaviors may include physically aggressive actions such as hitting, jerking, yelling and shouting.   Such behaviors drive thick wedges of resentment and antagonism into the relationship, fracturing it and creating great stress which may ultimately be heartbreaking. Some of these behaviors, such as ignoring, can be very subtle. Some are disguised as jokes and sarcasm. We don't always see the effects right away. All of the behaviors show a lack of caring, disinterest in, and disrespect for the other.

Many years ago a friend of mine was wrapping gifts at my home. When she finished, she asked me if I wanted to keep the long cardboard tube on which the gift wrap had been rolled. I had just gotten a new puppy, Thomas Edison.

Well, I was delighted! The cardboard tube was light enough to bat the puppy on the hinder when he misbehaved, without hurting him. Or so I thought! A few minutes later Thomas Edison wandered past, enroute to check out something that had fallen behind the bookcase. As he wiggled into the space between the bookcase and the wall, I tapped the tube on his rump and hollered "No!" Tom spun about, eyes wide and riveted on mine. Sometimes a dog looks at us in a way that changes our lives forever. I saw surprise, fright and deep hurt in his face. My mouth dropped open and I took a step backward. The anguish in his eyes brought tears to mine as I dropped the tube and scooped him into my arms. I spent the next half-hour apologizing and crying over him.

Tom taught me an unforgettable lesson about fear, aggression, power and control. It was the beginning of my awareness that the habit/expectation paradigm governing my relationships with dogs, and perhaps others in my life, needed to change, because it caused me to meet my needs in ways that were destructive. I burned that cardboard tube.

Is Altruism a Need?

Social animals form relationships to satisfy mutual and respective needs in a reciprocal fashion. In addition to the category of behaviors termed *reciprocal*, another category of behaviors called *altruistic* may be found in communities. Altruism is described as satisfying a need to help another with no expected or anticipated return on one's investment, that is to say, *without* reciprocity. Altruism thus appears one-sided, placing no demands on the beneficiary. There are many observed incidents of altruism among social species. Because of its extent, some have argued that engaging in altruistic acts is a need of members of social species, and that this need may even be encoded in their genes.

One of my dogs, Kiwi, exhibited some apparently altruistic behavior which I can't explain in any other terms.

My old dog, Capa, had mast cell cancer which would, in a few weeks, take her from this world. It was November: deer hunting season. Local hunters had met with success, leaving us piles of entrails to deal with. I let the dogs out for the night, going out with them as usual to keep them from wandering off. Kiwi faded into the blackness, ignoring my calls to come. About 20 minutes later I heard him bound onto the front porch and went to let him in. His abdomen was very distended, and I suspected he had found a pile of deer innards and stuffed himself. He paced around for a few minutes, then walked over to where Capa lay on her bed and regurgitated the entire mass right under her nose. While I wasn't impressed with the smelly cleanup, I had cause for reflection. He could have upchucked anywhere. Why did he do it right in front of her? He wasn't particularly hungry, having eaten just a couple of hours before; why would he so deliberately head for a food source? And since he was out roaming, why not stay out and roam a little longer, since it was an activity that he enjoyed when he got the chance? Why come directly

> *back? Did he have a sense, or perhaps even know, that Capa was sick? Did he want to participate in her care by bringing her food? I'll never know the answers. But based on so many other observations of animals behaving altruistically, I believe it's probable that's what Kiwi was doing.*

If we are all related, as Native Americans and quantum physics maintain, what we do to one we do to another. Thus, committing an altruistic act would help not only the beneficiary, but the benefactor in some way, and this result, according to biologist Rupert Sheldrake, would resonate through the entire system. Is altruism, then, so hard to accept as a need that may be satisfied through relationship? In fact, relationship is implicitly assumed and explicitly made manifest in the commission of altruistic acts. And maybe non-human beings as well as humans have a need to just feel good because they've done something that helped someone else.

Sheldrake suggests that if dogs and people help each other to survive, they are genetically co-dependent, retaining this co-dependency over many generations. According to Darwinian laws, they would thus have been subject to selection for interspecies altruism. By virtue of our altruistic and empathetic tendencies, as well as our apparent capacities to feel shame and remorse, I would again argue that we and our dogs are indeed equals. Acceptance of this argument fundamentally changes the way we relate to each other, as well as the subsequent order we establish.

****

Reflections . . .

1. We create relationships to satisfy needs and desires.
2. Several different types of relationships are possible.
3. All things created are related.

4. The power of relationship is stronger than a relationship based on power.
5. We behave as we believe.
6. Relationships require limits.
7. Eliminate behaviors that cause fear in others.
8. Strive to meet needs creatively and nondestructively.
9. Interspecies altruism may be in our genes.

Brothers and Sisters, I bid you beware

Of giving your heart to a dog to tear.

-- Rudyard Kipling

4 Order

order \'ord-ər\ to put things into their proper places in relation to each other.

facilitated by: respect

Who's in Charge?

In every relationship, someone needs to be in charge of setting limits. Who is in charge depends upon the situation. For example, I'm in charge of keeping my dog at home rather than allowing him to roam the countryside. Roaming is in a dog's nature. I clearly need to be in charge here, setting the limits that control expression of the roaming instinct. Refusing to set and acknowledge limits disrespects both individual and relationship.

Concerning the amount of time required for any individual dog's needs to be met and satisfied, the dog's in charge. I learn, for example, that my Labrador needs at least one hour of hard exercise daily to meet his need for physical movement and sensory stimulation. Sometimes I learn this the hard way. On those days I can't provide at least this hour of exercise, I may come home to find a pillow in pieces on the floor. If I respect the dog's needs for certain things, order can be established. Unrespected and subsequently unmet needs create behavior issues as animals search for ways to get their needs satisfied. As we disrespect their needs, so also will they disrespect ours.

The Conditions of Limits

Order thrives when appropriate limits are set, establishing a stable yet flexible structure which encourages exploration, learning, development, growth and play. Order decays when limits are too restrictive, nonexistent, or arbitrary.

Several conditions are possible with respect to limits. On one extreme are *inflexible limits.* They must always be respected, and consequences for not doing so are severe. The environment with inflexible limits is characterized by military discipline, where rules are set down for all to see, and consequences, whether positive or negative, predictably follow actions. On the other extreme is the condition of *no limits.* No-limit conditions are often characterized by chaos. There is a third condition of *arbitrary limits,* where the rules change constantly, but only the enforcer knows what the rules are or when the change will happen. There is a certain amount of chaos in this condition as well. A fourth condition is *balanced limits,* where the need for structure is balanced with a certain amount of freedom, and that balance is determined by the needs and abilities of the individuals in the relationship. This fourth condition provides predictable consequences and a certain amount of flexibility. It minimizes chaos, and, unlike the other three conditions, allows individuals (dog or human) to exercise a great deal of control over their own destiny.

The most damaging condition for the order and stability of a relationship is a condition of arbitrary limits. Based on the whims of the enforcer, this condition is akin to an abuse of power. If order has been established, it will not long endure in an environment where rules change frequently and unpredictably. When dogs can't form logical associations or patterns between their actions and the consequences of their actions, a state of learned helplessness may develop. Animals refuse to even try, because their appropriate actions have been inconsistently reinforced, and inappropriate actions have been punished in a non-contingent manner. The unpredictable environment may erode confidence, diminish self-esteem, and retard learning and development. It can also establish aggressive behaviors. The condition of arbitrary limits is characterized by chaos rather than order. It is ubiquitous in our world, and a major cause of behavior problems in our dogs and ourselves.

We often inadvertently find ourselves in a condition of arbitrary limits with our dogs because it can be hard to understand or manage the needs of another species. It's also hard to know and use the appropriate response on the spur of the moment. Besides our dogs, we may find ourselves in this condition with regard to ourselves, our children, and other humans with whom we relate.

The condition of no limits may be equally as chaotic as arbitrary limits, though less dramatic. Many people believe, for instance, that dogs with behavior problems will benefit from a move to a "farm" with unlimited room to run and behave as they please. As idyllic as it sounds, no social animal can have a fulfilling existence in such an environment because it fails to take into account the very thing that makes us social: cooperative interaction.

More desirable, but not optimal, is the condition of inflexible limits, which at least creates a predictable environment. Once everyone learns the rules – which dogs often need to do by painful trial and error because of their inability to read or completely interpret the spoken word – things settle into a stable, albeit not very stimulating existence, perhaps not unlike a laboratory or some training kennels.

Setting limits is a skill. We are not born with this skill, and need to learn it.

An effective and simple strategy for learning to set limits is a *learn-to-earn* program. This can also become the basis on which we learn to communicate with our dogs in useful ways that get both our needs met. Communication provides clarity, allowing us to move into the fourth condition of balanced limits.

The concept of learn-to-earn was formalized by veterinarian Victoria Voith in 1977. Many variations have evolved, but the end result is the same: self-inhibition of impulsive behavior. When individuals learn and subsequently choose to self-inhibit their impulses with consistent results, relationships benefit because anxiety and ambiguity decrease, while predictability and safety increase. The ability to consistently make choices that create positive outcomes increases self-esteem and preserves order.

Learn-to-earn programs are based on operant learning, a behavioral construct which is understood by creatures as diverse as cockroaches and Cocker spaniels. Dog does a good thing, dog gets a good thing. Dog does a bad thing, dog loses a good thing. These are called positive reinforcement and negative punishment, respectively, and through experience individuals learn to make choices that provide expected outcomes, controlling their impulses to do inappropriate things because they know the penalty is losing something they value. In practice, for example, I ask all my dogs to sit before opening the door for them to go outside, and to exit only when their name is called (positive reinforcement). If anyone gets up before their name is called, they are put in a down/stay until the other dogs have exited; they get to go last (negative punishment). There are many resources available for learn-to-earn programs.

Limits and the exercise of power can also become less arbitrary when we appreciate and accept that those over whom we presume to have power have feelings. Great teachers understand that their students have feelings. This applies to human as well as non-human students. Not only can feelings similar to our own be attributed to dogs, but individual dogs will have quite individual feelings and express them in individual ways. Unless we are sadistic, it's not easy to treat with insensitivity an individual whom we know may react with fear, frustration, embarrassment or confusion. Since behavior is motivated by feelings, what do practices that create these feelings in our animals say about us? With insights into our dogs' feelings, we can more easily refrain from using power arbitrarily, creating an environment which is orderly because of its predictability and fairness.

There are dogs who seem to do just fine under conditions of arbitrary limits, inflexible limits, and no limits. But perhaps limits that seem arbitrary, absent or inflexible to one individual appear balanced to another. This demonstrates the importance of engaging your dog. It's the only way you can learn what conditions are best for that individual animal.

Observe your dog in a variety of situations to discover what condition of limits works best for him, as well as when it's appropriate to allow him to set the limits. I think it's important to allow our dogs to participate in setting limits, because when any individual has the ability to self-determine her course, the act of self-determination is empowering and self-actualizing. In order to be whole, every individual, even non-human ones, needs to have a measure of influence over self and environment. Without this influence, a variety of neuroses and psychoses can develop. Stereotypies such as cribbing, for example, are common in horses kept confined to stalls or other too-small, impoverished environments. Aggression and anxiety are seen in zoo animals kept in confined, unstimulating environments, and may result in failure to nurture young and harassment or killing of cage mates.

We Are What We Do

An orderly environment serves another function. How many humans approaching retirement are terrified at the prospect of no longer working in an occupation to which they have devoted a major part of their lives? What are they to do with all the time on their hands? Few things increase self-worth like gainful employment. If our work is valued, we are valued. For our work to be valued, we need to follow a disciplined and orderly approach which allows us to learn and practice competence in the skills that attribute value to the work we are doing. Many dogs have lost the jobs they were bred to do. Dogs, like humans, identify and become their role. When the role no longer exists, identity can be lost and self-worth shattered. The role of companion is different than the role of shepherd, rescuer, hunter, guard, or other diverse jobs that dogs were bred to do for us, and which allowed for freer and appropriate expressions of their instinctive behaviors. The role of companion dog requires different skills, one of which is inhibition of instinctive behavior. Dogs may readily learn these different skills when a disciplined approach is taken. The learn-to-earn program provides an entry-level position for a dog learning the occupation of companion animal.

Self-inhibition of impulsive behavior is one of the core requirements for an orderly community. Learn-to-earn programs work because both we and our dogs participate in setting limits. If you don't already have a learn-to-earn program in place, and your dog is not as self-inhibited as you would like, I encourage you to begin such a program. This can be as simple as asking for brief (2-3 seconds) eye contact preceding the delivery of anything your dog gets from you. All dogs should learn to check in frequently with their humans by giving brief eye contact. It is an acknowledgment of connection and an expression of respect and reciprocity.

Out of Respect

Some say dogs wish to please us. Others argue dogs are incapable of this, and that their apparent desire to please is only a biological urge to be in the most comfortable, least energy consuming state. The argument continues that by "pleasing" us they ingratiate themselves to us, so we don't make them exert too much energy performing meaningless (to them) activities such as coming when called, sitting, or heeling, when what they'd prefer to do is express their instinctive desires to do other more meaningful things. I think this argument vastly underestimates, and is perhaps even in denial about, the role our companion dogs play in our lives. What makes the most sense to me is building a respectful and fulfilling relationship with our dogs because the end result of this seems to be a dog who is so much more willingly compliant with our wishes. The reciprocity of this arrangement reduces reactive, chaotic behavior and promotes order and stability.

Many indigenous cultures believe that to be respected, one must first show respect. This applies to dogs as well as humans. Our dogs' behavior will reflect our behavior. How do we demonstrate respect for our dogs? In the book *Veterinary Aromatherapy*, author Nellie Grosjean relates a poem called A Dog's Prayer, which sets forth many ways of showing respect, such as lifetime commitment, forgiveness of housetraining mistakes, affection and food; but above all is the dog's plea: "Please, I beseech you, never abandon me! Never abandon me!"

A relationship based on respect and reciprocity meets needs more effectively, and more lovingly, than a relationship based on power and control. Respect and reciprocity create a framework of equality. The need for respect is a great equalizer, bridging the gap between and among species.

To merit equality, one must respect and trust the other. Based on trust and respect, equals do things for each other without asking questions about motives or consequences. They have faith that what the other is asking is somehow important, and simply feel good about cooperating to meet the other's need. Cooperating is a self-reinforcing act; it has its own rewards. This arrangement requires faith that the trust will not be abused through requests for unreasonable things. Is this what we mean when we say dogs want to please us?

To take this a step further, sometimes dogs do things for us that we don't ask. They seem to have a sense of how their behavior will affect an outcome, and appear unmindful of negative consequences to themselves. Out of respect, trust, and what many call love, dogs do things that don't work for them, but do work for others. I recently watched a documentary which described an account of a dog flinging her body in front of a car to prevent it hitting a child in the road.   An act like this is far removed from the ideas of hierarchy, dominance or leadership. It can perhaps be explained by respect, trust, and above all, concern for another's welfare. Beyond reciprocity is self-sacrifice and altruism.

The Role of Status

Status often equates to dominance in our lives with dogs, and dominance is associated with hierarchy. While it's true that in some social groups (wolf packs for example) there is a breeding pair of high-status individuals to which others defer, so-called dominance hierarchies in social groups are often fluid to the point where it's difficult, and sometimes impossible, to say who gets to wear the label "alpha." Status and dominance are actually two quite different things. Legitimate status – that which can be respected – has to do with accomplishment. Dominance, on the other hand, is about overpowering a perceived rival for access to preferred, and possibly scarce, resources. Dominance is about competition. Status is not about competition. Status is about competence, which earns respect from those who admire competence. I very much like the expression of admiration that author and psychoanalyst Jeffrey Masson puts forth in *When Elephants Weep*, with respect to wolves displaying admiration for the "alpha" animals in their group, admiration being a combination of deep affection and respect.

Affection and respect order relationships because they are the foundation for learning. Try learning from someone you have no respect for. Is it easy? But learning from someone you admire is often nearly effortless. It may even be uplifting. What causes our dogs to develop affection, respect and admiration for us, to the point where they hang on our every word and gesture? I've found fun, consistency, and fairness at the top of the list. I often glance up to see Diamond gazing at me softly, and if I had to name what I see in her eyes, I would call it admiration, at least. I also call it love. I am deeply humbled.

Defining the Reality of Order

In their extensive studies of canine genetics and behavior, psychologists John Paul Scott and John Fuller observed that pups engaged in *allelomimetic* behavior, copying the behaviors of others in their groups, as early as five weeks of age. Behavior is part of the culture of a group. Copying the behavior of others is *enculturation:* learning the practices of a social group resulting in one becoming accepted into and identifying with that group. Group acceptance provides us with psychological if not physical safety.

Animals engage in allelomimetic behavior as a way of adapting to their environment. Adaptation promotes survival. By copying the behavior patterns of others, we appear more like them. We fit in by learning and conforming with the behaviors that our social group finds acceptable.

Allelomimetic behavior is facilitated by maintaining contact through hearing, sight and touch, and Scott and Fuller concluded that it is fundamental to a dog's social life. The types and degrees of sensory interactions that are shared by individuals in a group affect the emotions and behavior that will develop, subsequently influencing the culture of the group and whether or not individual animals fit into it. Fitting in means our behaviors, and those of other members of our group, are consistent and predictable, creating a safer environment.

Dogs are able to observe, interpret and act upon the gestures made by a human. Thus a dog will follow the pointing finger of a human to find a hidden toy, piece of food or other treasure, or learn how to negotiate an obstacle by watching a human negotiate it. She will also follow the gaze of a human to a target, or one bowing or nodding toward a target. Remarkably, inexperienced dog puppies were nearly as good at these tasks as adults. This ability of dogs has vast implications for the way we relate to and teach them. In the Tellington Method, a "wand" (dressage riding whip) is used as an extension of the arm to direct a dog through the Confidence Course, a practice supported by this research.

Our dogs watch, touch and listen to us constantly. Researchers have found that dogs have the ability to learn just by watching and listening, that they change their behaviors in response to whether or not we are paying attention to them, and that their learning curve and ability to perform a task are about the same whether they are taught the task through operant conditioning or observational learning. Despite the cleverness of dogs, they may misinterpret our actions and intent, possibly with serious consequences. Mindful that we are always being observed, one of our major responsibilities toward our dog is to behave in consistent and predictable ways, setting the example we want her to follow. This defines for the dog the reality of order in the relationship.

Can your dog depend on you to behave in predictable and consistent ways? Is your behavior unpredictable or erratic? If we behave in confusing, indecisive, or inconsistent patterns, our dogs can't depend on us to set a proper example for them. This is disorderly and fosters instability in the relationship because it threatens safety and security. The dogs lose their anchor. Why should they sit calmly with their food in front of them until told to take it, if sometimes we let them lose all self-control and knock the dishes from our hands? As I work with clients, I find a basic issue is how to help them become more predictable in their behavior, so the dogs know the "game." Most dogs are happy to play our good, consistent behavior game when the rules are clear.

> *Harriett was determined to teach her energetic Boston Terrier Molly the art of self-control. Through many repetitions, and with Harriett's patient coaching, Molly learned that sitting and staying was the best way to get the things that were important to her. But it wasn't only patience and repetition that accomplished the task.*
>
> *Molly's "school" started at the same time each day. And everything she got was earned by sitting and staying briefly. Harriett and Molly ate their meals together. Molly learned to sit calmly in front of her full dish until Harriett finished prayers over the food. Harriett herself was a model of predictability and consistency.*

Harriett's job was perhaps a little easier because she was the only human member of the household. When there's more than one person in the family, *The Good Behavior Game* gets harder to play because, often, not every family member or caretaker follows the rules consistently. And sometimes it's even hard to agree on what the rules should be. As you can imagine, such a situation is extremely confusing for the dog, who then has no consistent model to follow.

Watching and listening to humans behave in consistent and predictable ways increases the probability that the dog will behave consistently and predictably, because such an environment reduces stress and reactivity. If, for example, we teach our dog that any time a door is approached, the way to get to go through it is to sit and wait to be invited through, the dog learns that a sit of some duration will always be expected in front of any door, and may even take initiative to sit without being asked. We teach this not because we are leaders, but because it is safer, and it is polite and respectful. For my dogs, this rule predictably applies not only to our home environment, but to all doors everywhere: crates, boarding kennel, groomer, vet, pet store and car. Predictability builds trust, and the best relationships are always based on trust.

Can we take such an environment too far? Is there such a thing as too consistent and too predictable? I believe there is. A rigid, institutionalized environment allows little, if any, space for creativity, imagination and growth. This may eventually destabilize the relationship; it's just not fun or stimulating any more.

More study needs to be done on the effects of human personalities and behaviors on behavior problems in dogs. Ethicist James Serpell relates several anecdotes that appear to support a correlation, but not always in ways we would expect. For example, a neurotic human may generate nervous behavior in her dog, but not because the dog is following her example. Rather, the dog misbehaves because the neurotic human creates an unpredictable and unsafe environment, which increases the dog's anxiety, and the state of anxiety causes misbehavior. There may, however, be a direct linkage. I often wonder how many problem behaviors are the direct result of dogs seeing these behaviors in their homes. Puts a whole new slant on biting, doesn't it?

Learn from Mistakes

Nobody's perfect and mistakes sometimes get made. Are mistakes okay? Absolutely, but only if we learn from them. This involves mindfulness. Mindless, repetitive mistakes are irresponsible, undermine the order we're trying to create, and, in fact, carry the implicit assumption that we prefer chaos. But don't feel guilty about occasional lapses. As I say to my clients when they confess their indiscretions, "How human of you!"

Use your mistakes to sharpen your focus. Practice positive self-talk: "I made a mistake, but I'll do better next time." Get over it and get back on track. I try to get clients to express any feelings they may have about their role in creating their dogs' issues, and to accept what they may have done as part of a learning process that brought them to this point of change. Then I encourage them to take any energy they were putting into guilt or resistance and use it to work with their dog. I stress to them the importance of realizing that, whatever happens, they get to make the choices that determine the outcomes. Thus we move forward into a more positive space where learning from mistakes is enabled and supported.

Just as dogs change what doesn't work for them, let your desire for order and stability guide you to make changes in what works for you. If your dogs begin to misbehave on a consistent basis, instead of asking, "What's wrong with this dog?" ask, "What's not working here? What do *I* need to change?" Maybe there *is* something wrong with the dog. Many medical conditions can cause behavioral issues. But more often the answer is found by looking within ourselves first.

The Potential for Disorder

While systems seek stability, they are often in chaos. If we provide too much support for our dogs, we risk making them so dependent that they are anxious and insecure if we're not in sight, though some dogs seem to have a predisposition for extreme dependency and separation distress. Continually striving for perfection also makes us continually dissatisfied with our performance. It interferes with learning because it tolerates no mistakes. This could cause us to become tyrants, and tyrants are no fun! So we need to focus on the present: be as good as we can at this particular moment in time, and not worry whether it's perfect. Instead, are we accomplishing something we feel good about and having fun to boot?

I don't think there's anything more tedious for a dog than our tendency to demand blind obedience in every situation. Learn-to-earn programs, for example, can have flexibility, especially when dogs make good progress toward perfecting more appropriate behaviors. Relaxing a learn-to-earn program is acceptable when behavior is no longer an issue. The program can always be tightened up if the dog's behavior starts to regress. I also don't insist on always calling my dogs away from things they find interesting. This is an abuse of relationship, preventing them from satisfying their basic doggy needs to sniff and explore. To avoid rigidity, I participate. I go along. See what I might discover with my dogs leading me along the path of exploration!

So now we've got our relationship ordered, and it's ticking along like a well-tuned car. Are we done? Not even close! Still in the driveway!

Overconfidence can sabotage the most well-ordered of relationships. It can lead to cockiness, poor judgment and insensitivity to the situation. My dog Kiwi taught me an important lesson about overconfidence.

Kiwi had lived in a shelter for seven years and had never learned a recall. In fact, if I even raised my voice to him he went the other direction. So to begin his recall training, I had him wear a very long rope whenever we went on walks. I held the end of it. After a few weeks he appeared to recognize his name and had learned to stay closer to me. In fact he got so good at this that I was fooled into thinking he had indeed learned a recall, and had developed enough skill and trust to do it when asked.

So one day we left the rope behind. For awhile Kiwi stayed close and I thought all was well. Then he spied something interesting across the river. He jumped in, swam to the other side and ran through the cow pasture. No amount of shouting could get his attention, in fact, it accelerated his flight. After a few minutes I quit shouting. I waded across the river, threaded myself through the electric fence, and got a jolt that would stun a heifer. Then I lost a shoe in eighteen inches of manure-laced muck and left pieces of flesh in a tangle of blackberry brambles. I finally cornered Kiwi in the barnyard, while several dozen Holstein heifers looked on, an expression on their placid faces which I swear was smugness.

Meanwhile Thomas Edison and Sand had followed me across the river, getting themselves soaked and covered in manure. We all took an alternate route back through two acres of composted manure, where at least there were no electric fences. My ego in shreds along with my skin, I spent the rest of the day in a foul mood, bathing and deodorizing all three dogs and seriously questioning my judgment.

Such situations can be avoided by staying open to what I call "situational feedback," being mindful of what's happening from moment to moment. Had I been watching Kiwi carefully, I would have been ready with a distraction when he got too interested in whatever lured him across the river.

He wore his rope some months longer. It took a year and a half, but Kiwi learned to come when I called 95% of the time. I think that's pretty good for an old dog who'd never been trained. In the process he helped me learn the skills of patience, creativity and forgiveness.

Say "Thank You!"

One thing I'd love to see more often is for us to say "Thank you!" to our dogs. Maybe my dogs don't understand the concept of giving thanks, but it makes me feel good to express to them my gratitude for their respect and cooperation. When I combine the words with gentle eye contact and touch, I am fulfilling their need for social contact and recognition. I'm also recognizing the partnership we've achieved, and the reciprocity of the relationship that serves our mutual needs.

* *

Reflections . . .

1. Who's in charge depends on the situation.
2. No is not enough.
3. Learn-to-earn programs allow both dogs and humans to participate in setting limits.
4. We are what we do.
5. Reciprocity determines the nature of a relationship.
6. Trust and respect are more helpful than power and control.
7. Dogs are always watching and listening to us.
8. Mistakes are part of the learning process.
9. Change what's not working.
10. Systems seek stability but are often in chaos.
11. Say "thank you" to your dog.

We keep our power
by protecting the power of others
— Thomas Moore.

5   Stability

stability \stə-'bil-ət-ē\ 1a: the strength to stand or endure.

facilitated by: balance

Expanding the Limits

Limits, if they are to contribute to the longevity of the relationship, must be balanced with freedom. Both limits and freedom should be based on the respective needs of the individuals in the relationship. When this balance is achieved, the relationship has the flexibility to endure; it is stable yet resilient.

What does stability allow us to do? It lets us relax and enjoy each other's company as we engage in mutual opportunities for exploration, learning, development, growth and play.

> *Penny, a Rottweiler mix, had lived in a Florida shelter for four years. The desperate shortage of resources in Penny's shelter prevented adequate socialization during her critical periods of puppy development. Adopted by a family from Wisconsin, Penny adjusted with difficulty, showing no impulse control, no frustration tolerance, and limited social skills toward both humans and other dogs. One day, while playing with a group of neighborhood dogs in an unfenced yard, Penny nipped a child who had walked past and taken an interest in the dogs' play. Fortunately Penny's human stepped in before serious damage occurred. When I met Penny for the first time, she looked me straight in the eye, hackles raised, head low, a growl in her throat.*

Penny's human, Sarah, was not only unhappy with Penny's antisocial behavior; she was also distressed because Penny had created a strong bond with Sarah's father Dean, who spent a lot of time playing with her. Penny was supposed to be Sarah's dog, a graduation gift from her parents. The fact that Penny would not bond with her, and virtually ignored her, made Sarah very unhappy and somewhat jealous of her dad, especially since Sarah had worked with Penny at the shelter where she volunteered while going to college.

Dean was an outgoing and gregarious person. He took care of Penny while Sara was finishing school. He clearly enjoyed life, and from his appearance and the way he interacted with Sarah, I suspected he set few limits for himself or others. Sarah's mother, Anne, seemed to have most of the authority in the family. I helped them do some goal-setting within two specific areas.

- *First, teaching Penny to behave appropriately and safely in social situations.*
- *Second, helping Penny to bond with Sarah, whom she would live with once Sarah moved out on her own.*

Our treatment plan included rigid adherence to a learn-to-earn program. I emphasized to Dean the need to provide Penny with structure rather than indulging her and giving in to both their impulses, which involved rough play and no consequences for Penny's willful behavior. I also asked Dean if he would be comfortable relinquishing his caregiver role to Sarah, who would become responsible for feeding, walking and other maintenance. Dean agreed to this reluctantly. Penny's attentions and boisterous behavior pleased him.

Within three months the first goal had been achieved. Penny was even beginning to show a friendly interest in people toward whom she had previously taken an active dislike, such as Sarah's friend Gail, who had taken the time to learn how to control some of her own behaviors that were triggers for Penny. The family was starting to relax, believing Penny was out of the danger zone in terms of the liability her aggressive behavior had created. But Sarah still didn't feel she had made a connection with Penny. Despite her stellar compliance with the treatment plan, she was still just a caregiver to Penny. We talked about what Dean had done to win Penny's heart, and decided play was the answer. They had fun together. But, wondered Sarah, if I play with her, will she think I'm relaxing the limits? Will the aggressive, unsocial, unrestrained Penny return?

The learn-to-earn program and other elements of the treatment plan had been effective in instilling socially appropriate behaviors. One goal, the family's need for a safe environment, had been satisfied. It was time to address the second goal, a fulfilling relationship between Sarah and Penny. We needed to convince Penny that Sarah could meet her social needs as well as Dean. In return we hoped Penny would reciprocate and transfer her affections to Sarah, and through play this is exactly what began to happen. With Dean out of the picture, someone had to satisfy Penny's social needs, and playing with Sarah did this beautifully. Integrating learn-to-earn into play sessions kept things from getting out of balance. I reassured Sarah that if any of Penny's behavior problems seemed to worsen with the play strategies, she could always drop out the play, withdrawing attention from Penny for periods of time to gain her cooperation.

Dogs may generalize respectful behaviors across situations, and generalization increases stability. This expands the boundaries, and results in greater freedom of action. As one demonstrates a capacity to handle responsibility, one gains more freedom. This is true for humans; it can also be true for dogs.

All of my dogs were raised in a learn-to-earn paradigm. But I find them taking initiative to apply the lessons to situations that we never specifically addressed, such as going to bed. Thomas Edison, for example, always asks permission before getting on my bed if I'm there first. He approaches the bed and sits without being asked, watching me until I invite him up. I didn't teach him this. If anything, I would expect the opposite, jumping up unbidden, because when he was a tiny baby I carried him to bed to sleep with me, creating a nest for him among the pillows. Instead he chooses to wait for permission and, from the time he was strong enough to jump onto the bed by himself, has always done this. There is peace and harmony in such an orderly arrangement.

The Role of Influence

Taking initiative is influential. Influence exerts pressure on individuals and events to achieve certain outcomes. In the achievement of an outcome, limits exert influence depending on whether they are respected or ignored. Influence can support or undermine balance. We are influential regardless of whether we are proactive or reactive, mindful or mindless. Whatever approach or mindset we choose in a given situation will influence an outcome.

Influence and choice are closely bound. In order to make the choice that has the best chance of influencing a desired outcome, we need to do several things. First, we must realize we have a choice, and we always do. Second, we need to inform our choice by learning what we need to know to make the best one. Third, we need to exercise our right to choose, and many of us relinquish this right to someone we believe is better qualified. In actuality, no one is better qualified to make choices for us than ourselves. Failure to realize or accept that we have choices is also influential and will result in a certain outcome. Though we may choose to do nothing, we are still having an influence on a situation through our inaction.

I invited two colleagues to my house for lunch: Erica, a very confident, proactive and mindful woman, and Jenny, a reactive and somewhat mindless person who often let her emotions get the better of her. I asked if they'd like to meet my dogs.

Among the group of dogs were two adolescents about a year old: a visiting Golden Retriever named Bongo, and my dog, Sand. Both women were standing when the dogs came in. Kiwi and Thomas Edison sniffed the ladies' hands and left the room. Bongo and Sand approached Erica who stood her ground, petted them briefly, then looked away and resumed her conversation with me. Then they went to Jenny, who had been leaning against the couch. As the dogs approached, she backed further into the couch until it seemed she would climb right up onto the arm of it. Bongo and Sand pressed into her, testing to see how much space they could take from her. Jenny's body was inclined backward, her hands were up around her face, and it was clear she would have kept backing right into the corner and up the wall if the couch hadn't been in her way. Had she been another dog, she might have rolled onto her back and peed.

Jenny was completely intimidated. Her submissive behavior, which set no limits, made her a target for these two young dogs, intent on testing their social skills. In comparison, Erica's assertive behavior, which set limits, was neither intimidating nor inviting. Both women influenced the situation. Two different outcomes ensued, based on the choices each made in her approach and mindset. Erica's outcome was balance and stability, Jenny's unbalance and instability.

Though I later regretted my failure to intervene before the dogs backed Jenny into a corner, I was fascinated by the interaction. I did notice the warmth of our collegial relationship seemed to diminish following the apparently destabilizing nature of her experience.

Is the ability to give and receive influence determined by our genes? In the case of dog-human relationships, recent research seems to point to a genetic root. Dog puppies and adults demonstrated patterns of attachment to their owners and handlers (familiar humans) that wolf pups did not display.

Prior socialization had only a minor affect on attachment behavior directed toward the human caregiver. In fact, even socially deprived adult dogs showed attachment behavior with a small amount of interaction. Wolves, in comparison, even with intensive socialization, don't show the attachment patterns found in domesticated (pet) dogs.

One hypothesis suggests that socialization is a prerequisite for attachment to humans. Another indicates it may not be, and the authors of this study concluded that our dogs' attachment behavior performs the same function as for that of a human infant. Socialization is influential, creating a "scaffold" upon which complex relational behaviors may develop. A scaffold built upon appropriate limits, influence and choices, is stable yet flexible.

Individualizing the Approach

Just as every human is different, needing and setting different limits, so every dog is unique. When Diamond was a pup, she and her friends delighted in wrestling, and no matter how large the space, they always seemed to have the most fun and vigorous game under my chair, making it impossible for me to get within arms' reach of my keyboard. My limit-setting strategy was to say in a gruff, guttural voice something that sounded like "GHUHFF!" which stopped the action as effectively as a wet blanket. Order and stability restored, I looked about and noticed that Tom had disappeared. The approach that worked so well for the boisterous pups caused Tom to become anxious, undermining his emotional balance. Never in his life has Tom done anything that caused me to raise my voice to him. I found him in the bathroom, hiding behind the toilet.

Not every technique works for every dog. As described in the last chapter, balance is achieved by recognizing that there is no generic approach to setting limits. Individuals differ from each other, and may change from moment to moment as they respond to their internal and external environments.

Threats to Stability

The function of play is disputed. Play helps create cohesive bonds among individuals. Through play we may resolve our disputes, strengthen our relationships, increase our skills and self-confidence, enjoy one another's' company, have fun and relieve stress. One of the biggest threats to stability is lack of opportunities for playfulness and fun.

Consider, for example, puppies who are more precocious and playful than their humans are able or willing to manage, where every exploratory effort is met with an intervention. The human is constantly on edge, the edge sharpening in direct relationship to the intensity of the pup's efforts to satisfy its curiosity. The visit of such a pair to my classroom (which is an interesting place for a puppy) is a sequence of playful puppy approaches to interesting things thwarted by the human hovering over or running after the pup with arms outstretched, a worried expression, and often the word *no* on her lips. I do understand that this client's intent most likely is merely to insure that her dog makes a positive impression. But at what cost? This relationship is already on shaky ground. For young animals and adults alike, playful curiosity is a need that helps put meaning and order into our world as it takes out the scariness and uncertainty. When this need is unsatisfied, developmental disabilities may result, making it difficult or impossible for an individual, dog or human, to behave normally as an adult.

Play can be an indicator of stress, because stressed animals don't play. The absence of ability or willingness to play may indicate relational as well as physical stress. While adult dogs usually don't play with the intensity of pups, normal adults in stable relationships maintain an aspect of playfulness throughout their lifetimes. The day before he passed, with all the grace and speed his old body could muster, Kiwi greeted me with a bound and started a game of chase when I made a quick move in his direction. He was seventeen.

Besides lack of fun and playfulness, another threat to stability occurs when attraction is based on physical attributes such as size, cuteness, softness and helplessness. Attraction to the physical may create engagement that is short-lived because it is based on superficialities. When puppies' endearing characteristics transform into bigger, stronger, faster bodies and willful behavior that we can no longer contain simply by picking them up, the relationship destabilizes quickly. Many of these dogs become statistics.

Competition can destabilize relationships. A good boss manages his workers with awareness and insight, mindful of their individual peculiarities, to minimize competition and optimize collaboration. Those of us with multiple dogs do well to operate in a similar fashion. Multiple dogs in a home can spin relationship issues into a different dimension. As I tell my clients, when you have two dogs you don't just have two dogs. You have each dog separately, and then you have the two together with a completely different set of relationship dynamics. Managing these dynamics can be challenging, especially when the goal is to create stability without having anyone suffer the loss of their freedom to behave in ways that are meaningful to them. The competition between Sand and Diamond, for example, plays out in interesting ways, one of which is the way he reacts to my disciplining her.

Diamond is the huntress, and when she's on a scent nothing can distract her. The dogs are forbidden to cross roads without escort. Rabbits are not. Disregarding the rule, Diamond followed the rabbit across the road, deaf to my calls. I put Tom and Sand in a down/stay and went to retrieve her. When I brought her back on a leash, Sand got up and rushed toward her. His mouth was open, tongue hanging out, head down and swinging from side to side. He got within about six feet of us, made a pouncing motion followed by a U-turn, and bounced away while looking back over his shoulder at us. If I had to say what this sequence meant, it looked to me like he was saying to her something like, "Ha-ha, you got in trouble!" and it reminded me of the sing-song way children display pleasure at one of their peers being caught out.

> *At that moment, she wasn't in charge, and it appeared he couldn't miss the opportunity to point that out to her.*

Sand is the classic "alpha wanna-be." He masks his lack of self-confidence with displays of loud barking at passersby, and aggressive posturing toward other dogs, always resulting in an attempt to mount, particularly if the other dog is in any way submissive or infirm. We have worked on changing these things, but something we can't change is the presence of Diamond, the alpha bitch, who seems to bring out Sand's worst qualities.

As you can imagine, striking a harmonious balance between these two disparate personalities is challenging, and allowing them too much flexibility would have a negative impact on everyone.

Play with your dog everyday; let him choose the game as often as you do, and let him win some of the time. See the potential for perfection[2] that may be cloaked in a crooked ear or less than perfect leash manners. Create an environment of cooperation, one dog at a time.

The operations of engaging, relating, ordering and stabilizing are complex. To help remember the steps in the process, I use the word *eros*, which forms an acronym for them. In addition to being a helpful mnemonic device, *eros* offers insights into the relationships we share with our dogs.

The Concept of *EROS*

Regrettably my use of **eros** as an acronym is not an original idea. The Internet encyclopedia Wikipedia shows at least three other applications expressing particular collections of ideas: Extremely Reliable Operating System; Event Related Optical

---

[2] The phrase "potential for perfection" was originally used by Linda Tellington-Jones to describe a state in which pain and fear are released at the cellular level, the function of cells is activated, and cellular intelligence is awakened. This allows an animal to integrate mental, emotional and physical processes, enabling them to overcome many physical and behavioral problems.

Signal (a brain-scanning technique); Eelam Revolutionary Organisation of Students (a militant Tamil group). The passing of ages has corrupted the word's meaning, and in modern usage it describes some of our baser instincts. Its origins, however, don't reflect its modern usage.

The classical origins of **eros** derive from the Greek verb *eraw*, which means desiring or longing for something intensely enough that one is willing to actively pursue the object of desire. Objects of desire may be physical and emotional, but they also include intellectual desires like wisdom and knowledge, and spiritual desires such as connection and community. Theologian Thomas Moore stresses that if our chosen pursuits lack an element of the erotic they are probably not worth doing, because they fail to engage us at our deepest, most soulful level. This includes the relationships we pursue with our dogs.

Eros as used by the Greeks, at the time of Plato and Socrates, had positive connotations. Most of us profess a strong desire to actively pursue better relationships with our dogs. These relationships contain physical, emotional and intellectual components. We touch our dogs often, experience a variety of emotions with and because of them, and spend much time teaching and training them. We seek out animal communicators to help us discover where the souls of our lost companions reside. These are active pursuits, the intent of which is to increase the quality of relationship.

Words are symbols and representations of significant things in our environments, such as attitudes and values. Fragile and malleable, they are readily broken, bent and shaped to reflect changes in cultural attitudes and values. A peculiarity of language is that different words may mean different things in different times and cultures, and this peculiarity may interfere with our attempts at understanding, maybe closing our minds to new ideas and deeper insights. Consider the meaning of the word *dog*. Webster's Ninth New Collegiate Dictionary's first definition of the word is "a highly variable domestic mammal." Farther down the list are more unfortunate definitions: "a worthless person; one inferior of its kind; an unattractive girl or woman." Early Christian cultures idealized *dog* as guardian and priest. Arabic cultures demonize *dog* as pariah, an unclean parasite. Just as *dog* may have a diversity of meanings, so may *eros.*

I happened upon *eros* by chance (or perhaps not by chance; there are no coincidences) while reading the work of psychologist Stanislav Grof. I was deep in the process of writing this book at the time, trying to put my ideas into an orderly pattern and not finding the key that would unlock the door to insight. Grof describes *eros* as the love instinct striving for union and the creation of higher units. As I read this again and again, considering and reflecting upon the pattern made up of e-r-o-s, I felt a resonance within me, and from that resonance came the order and pattern I was searching for:

> ❖   E – Engagement
> ❖   R – Relationship
> ❖   O – Order
> ❖   S – Stability

I looked through the lens of this pattern at the cases I was currently working with. In case after case I found myself asking a series of questions that could help organize the tangled dynamics of the issues:

> ❖ Is there more than a superficial attraction between individuals, creating the framework in which *engagement* can occur?
> ❖ To what degree is the client engaged with the dog?
> ❖ What is the quality of the *relationship*?
> ❖ Does the relationship contain the needed *order* to provide a foundation for stability?
> ❖ What is threatening the *stability* of the relationship enough for the client to seek professional help?
> ❖ Is there an instinct to love, respect and cooperate between *this* human and *this* dog?

When I posed the ideas and questions to clients, their expressions often became thoughtful and introspective. For many, this seemed a crossroads, possibly a very challenging one. What we do to others we also do to ourselves. Might the quality of relationship with our dogs indicate the quality of relationship with ourselves and others?

Socrates described a duality in *eros*.   One side of *eros* is concerned with the satisfaction of mental and rational needs, the other with emotional and physical needs. In a similar fashion, while *eros* describes the practices we can follow to improve our lives with our dogs, it also represents those less endearing characteristics we share: emotionality, reactivity, opportunism and self-interest, which may impede our efforts at relationship.   The practice of mindful dog teaching seeks to bring the duality of *eros*, which underlies all our relationships, into a state of balance and ultimately transcendence.

One of the defining criteria for life is the ability to procreate. Procreation requires union. Procreation need not refer only to the process of physical reproduction.   It may also include relationships, ideas, thoughts and intent, all of which can take on lives of their own, and through the process of synthesis constantly reproduce and reinvent themselves to create higher, more transcendent units. The best relationships occur between individuals who have no delusions about status, who are willing and able to concede and accept equality, and who do not engage in win-lose games of power and control. Instead of thinking of ourselves and our dogs in terms of alpha/omega, dominant/submissive, leader/follower, or other hierarchical terms, what if we think instead in terms of partners or companions, two individuals whose life paths have intertwined for a period of time, joining to share a common space and time, with the potential to achieve a synergy that either would find impossible or meaningless alone?   By engaging and relating as helpers and teachers, we rescue and uplift each other in the direction of our potential for perfection.

Toward the Creation of Higher Units

Ideas are the stuff of imagination. Ideas and imagination are given life through their application to actual situations. The life of the idea develops and grows through practice: repetition over time. And sometimes the idea becomes another thing entirely, when we become so good at practicing its application that we are able to take the idea apart and put it back together in previously unimagined patterns. This is the procreative aspect of **eros**, the "creation of higher units."

Part Two describes activities to help you practice **eros**. The activities are diverse. They may be as simple as sweeping your relaxed hand across your dog's body, or as complex as redecorating a room of your home. Just as a craftsperson needs tools to create a masterpiece, the activities will give you tools to craft a masterpiece of your relationship with your dog.

With mindfulness, regular and frequent practice over time becomes ritual, satisfying a deeper level of need, that of the mind, heart and soul for connection to something greater than one's self. Such connections may lead us to a sort of birthing process, where we awaken into an environment different from the one that precedes it. As you practice, be open to finding yourself in a new environment: the transcendent state of your relationship with your canine companion.

****

Reflections . . .

1. Stability requires balance between limits and freedom.
2. Influence can support or undermine desired outcomes.
3. We are the best qualified to make informed choices for ourselves.
4. We always have a choice.
5. Doing nothing is a choice.
6. Every individual is unique.
7. Play every day!
8. Attraction based on physical characteristics is not conducive to long-term stability.
9. Competition can destabilize relationships.
10. Engagement – Relationship – Order – Stability

A lot of growing up takes place between
"it fell" and "I dropped it."

-- Anon.

Part Two

6 Practice

7 Transcendence

6   *Practice*

practice \ 'prak-təs\ 1a. to perform or work at repeatedly so as to become proficient.

facilitated by: patience

The Potential for Change

Dogs and humans are not programmable machines that unthinkingly perform exactly the same maneuver many times in succession with perfect precision. A fatal flaw for so many of my clients is that their road to failure is paved with the good intentions to achieve precision and perfection, but without accepting that time and practice are required to develop these things. So recommendations are acted upon, but not nearly long enough for a new habit/expectation paradigm – that is, relating to our dog in a more useful way – to establish itself for the long haul. Nearly everyone asks, "How long will it take to fix or change (insert problem here)?" I'm limited to giving them probabilities. "If you do thus and so, and if your dog meets certain conditions (physical health, genetic profile, quality of life experiences, age, gender, etc.), on average expect to take four to six months to a year . . . And a colleague of mine worked on an issue for nearly five years before she was satisfied with the result." The only thing I can tell them with certainty is that if they practice, they will get better at something.

Even if what we get better at is not the particular thing we were aiming for, disciplined practice has the effect of structuring thought and emotional processes so that we generally make better, more informed and thoughtful choices; we become more mindful. Our habit/expectation paradigms become more plastic and expansive. This increased mindfulness may ripple into other situations. For example, becoming more mindful of what their dogs eat and how their diet may contribute to behavior issues often has the effect of causing clients to scrutinize their own eating practices.

During practice, two things are inevitable: mistakes and resistance. Embrace both as necessary parts of learning. It is indeed true that what doesn't kill us makes us stronger. So it is with mistakes and resistance. They are both part of the learningful process of practice and change, and are only detrimental when we ignore them. Go with the flow! On a trip to Hawaii I had the chance to snorkel the reef at Hanauma Bay. My companion and I swam through a gap in the reef to see the outer rim. The wave action created quite a suction through the gap and we were quickly sucked out into the bay. We watched the fish for awhile, and then had to go back in through that same gap. I could feel the combined oceanward pull of the waves and tide and briefly attempted to swim against it toward the shore. This was impossible. So I floated for a few minutes and watched the schools of fish around me. They were moving through the gap toward shore quite easily. The way they did it was to simply align themselves with the current, wait for a surge, then swim in with it. When the surge was going in the direction they didn't want to go, they simply did the fish equivalent of treading water. They never fought the current. Once I experienced the feel of what they were doing, it was so effortless. It meant being carried back a bit with each outbound wave, but swimming with the inbound wave more than made up for lost ground. Just like those fish, don't fight the current. Go with it. Let the resistance and mistakes be your teachers.

Practicing relationship with our dogs is easier when we have strategies, and strategies involving touch are very powerful due to the structure of the central nervous system. A major turning point in my practice was my introduction to the Tellington Method®. Becoming a practitioner of this method was nothing short of transformative.   Such is the power of mindful touch.

Circles

They come in many shapes – spirals, cones, tubes, balls. As I reflected on the multitude of circular manifestations in our perception, one shape particularly strikes me as representative of *eros*. This is the circle scribed by the hand in the Tellington Method®.

We engage the animal when we gently and lightly place our hand in contact with her fur. Relationship begins when we press lightly into the skin, scribing the circle of one and one-quarter revolutions, setting in motion the cascade of events that allow the animal's brain waves to entrain with ours. Upon completion of the circle we pause. Linda Tellington-Jones, the developer of the Tellington Method, has termed this event "PAWS," an acronym for "pause awakens wondrous stillness." It's during this pause and stillness that order is created. I have often watched animals become still during this pause, as if they were listening, watching or feeling carefully for something. I believe that it is during this time of stillness that a re-ordering of neurological function may happen, enabling subsequent changes in emotional state and behavior that are the hallmark of the Tellington Method.   Stability is created through our connection of the circles, either sliding from one to the next in straight lines, or finishing with long strokes over the animal's entire body. Methods such as this, which strengthen the body-mind connection, are empowering through their gentle ability to promote positive change, not only in the one receiving the touch, but also in the one giving it. Touching our dogs in mindful and meaningful ways helps us practice the engagement, relationship, order and stability that support an enduring bond.

Origins

Understanding the origins of bodywork such as the Tellington Method is important to help us appreciate the value of these methods in helping us to practice and sustain cooperative relationships with our companion animals. Bodywork in general, and the Tellington Method in particular, acknowledges the existence of emotions; indeed, this principle is an underpinning of the work. Both human and non-human animals have and express emotional states. Bodywork is a powerful experiential technique which allows us to access emotions at the cellular level. Focused bodywork, coupled with controlled breathing, provides a powerful technique which allows us to access a diversity of emotions and experiences, both past and future. It also opens the door to connecting with our animal companions at a cellular, molecular and energetic level.

The embryo has three primitive germ layers, the outermost of which is called the ectoderm. Cells in the ectoderm differentiate through various organizers into many different structures:
- epidermis, the outermost layer of the skin;
- claws, hair and glands of the skin;
- the nervous system including the brain;
- the mucus membranes of the mouth.

Among other things, the skin and mucus membranes are sensory organs, collecting stimuli from the environment and sending them to the brain for processing. The body-mind connection may be explained in part by these common roots of the skin and central nervous system, and may explain why mindful touch and bodywork so profoundly affect emotional states, as well as their resultant behaviors.

Cells have memory. When we touch the skin, we touch its cells. Are we also touching the memory of the brain in those cells?

Besides circular touches in the Tellington Method, we also find a system of exercises derived from Feldenkrais bodywork. These subtle and gentle exercises known as "Leg Circles" help to integrate the movements of systems of structures such as joints and muscles, influencing proprioceptive responses and use of alternative neural pathways. While done predominantly on legs, these movements can be done on any joint that articulates, even those which no longer have this capability, such as the fixed joints of the skullbones. The result is a positive change in function of that particular structural system, for example, more efficient movement of a leg, jaw, etc. Movement is basic to learning. Psychologist and educator Howard Gardner ascribes part of our intelligence to kinesthetics, how the body moves, and animal scientist Temple Grandin suggests that physical movement and the stimuli it made available was probably responsible for the evolution of the brain. When an elemental change in movement is made with awareness, sensory and motor areas of the brain are fundamentally reorganized, resulting in improved function of the entire organism. A corresponding positive change in emotional state and behavior is often seen.

A scientific basis for the effects of leg circles is found in the work of psychiatrist Wilhelm Reich, which has been further developed by therapists Alexander Lowen and John Pierrakos into an approach called *bioenergetics.* Bioenergetics uses a range of exercises including breathing, postures, movements and direct manual intervention, such as placing a dog's body into an organized and balanced posture to help the animal experience the feeling of organization and balance. This demonstrates to the dog that she is *able to be* in an organized and balanced frame, resulting, with time and practice, in an animal who actively places herself in an organized and balanced frame. At dog shows I offer Tellington TTouch bodywork, and many exhibitors take advantage of this service.

> *At a recent event, a breeder brought her Afghan hound to me. This dog had been traumatized at a show eight months earlier when he escaped from his pen to run free about the show grounds. He had been captured with a flying tackle from behind. Any approach from behind was now aversive, and the dog's tail was permanently tucked, making attempts at showing futile. Not only would the dog not stack, but he would also pivot around the handler to prevent any attempts by the judge to work behind him.*

While I worked with him, I tried to relax him enough to accept gentle manipulation of his tail into the natural upright position, and to appreciate that climbing up his handler like a rat up a drainpipe was not a functional behavior. As I did this, I talked to him, explaining to him that I thought he was a very brave dog for letting me work with him, and showing him that it was indeed possible to have his tail in a different position. I also suggested that this would be a very good way for him to carry himself in the ring. He was markedly relaxed after ten minutes of work. I asked his handler to let me know how his class went.

Later that afternoon she and her dog visited my booth with a second place ribbon in hand. He had carried his tail aloft through most of the class, until some distraction caused him to again tuck it. He also stood calmly for the judge. It was his first placing since the incident eight months previous. I got a big hug from his handler. She was close to tears in her joy.

Edie Jane Eaton, a Tellington Method instructor, elegantly described the power of this work, particularly when body wraps[3] are applied:

> We need to not overlook the influence of the
> wrap on the posture, the posture on the sense
> of self, and the sense of self on the behaviour.
> A big part of it all, I believe.

Here the body-mind connection comes very much into play, because what the body experiences is reflected in emotions and thought processes. As a result, changes in physical organization and balance are commonly accompanied by

---

[3] A half body wrap is applied to a dog by placing an elastic bandage around the body in a double figure-8: across the chest, crossed over the withers, crossed again under the ribs, and secured at the lumbar region of the back. It has the effect of gently pulling and pushing the body into symmetry and balance, enhancing the dog's sense of his own body and increasing his confidence. See *Getting in TTouch With Your Dog* (References) for more information.

dramatic changes in emotions and behavior. I routinely place wraps on nervous animals during consultations, often receiving comments from clients such as, "I'm amazed! I've never seen him so relaxed!"

Environment

Another strategy involves some fascinating research by Masaru Emoto, Doctor of Alternative Medicine. Dr. Emoto began his work measuring wave fluctuations in water, and ultimately developed photographic techniques which allowed him to image water crystals. Different types of water, tap water compared to natural spring water for example, form very different crystals. Some water is so compromised with foreign substances like chlorine and other pollutants that it forms no crystals at all. A most remarkable finding was that even words on a label attached to a vial of water influenced the type of crystal formed. Thus water labeled with "love and thanks" formed beautiful complete and intricate crystals resembling snow flakes. Water labeled with "you fool," however, formed no crystals. When music was played to a vial of water, the style of music influenced crystal formation. Organized patterns of classical melodies resulted in beautifully organized crystals. Disorganized, chaotic rock music resulted in incomplete, deformed crystals. This work suggests that water has the ability to copy and memorize information which it then displays in its crystal matrix. Living creatures such as humans and dogs are composed of about 70% water. If the qualities of words and music are reflected in the pattern of a water crystal, how might the sounds and words around us, which send vibrations through our watery selves, be reflected in our emotional states and behavior patterns? How might the sound of a dog's name affect emotions and behavior, both ours and the dog's?

My consultation room is a very pale shade of pink. Pale green and lavender rugs cover the floor. Green, lavender and pink throws and pillows cover the chairs. Music plays softly in the background. Lighting is incandescent and subdued. The air is lightly scented with cedar from the furniture and natural essential oils from a burning candle. Dogs enter this space without hesitation and are often reluctant to leave it. Humans relax in this space. Both lose some of the anxiety that gets in the way of learning new things.

Consider the environment in which you and your dog live and relate. Is your environment excessively loud or stimulating? Is the TV or some other electronic, sound-producing device constantly on? What about cell phones? Animals don't have the same filtering mechanisms in their brains as humans do; they can get a lot more aroused when overstimulated. Frankly, I don't think we handle this type of environment well either, and we're deluding ourselves into thinking we can multi-task to the extent that we do. Try turning off some of the noise in your dog's environment, substituting some quality music, or just plain silence. I prefer the sounds of Native American flute. And birdsong is lovely!

What colors do you surround yourself and your animal with? When given a choice, animals generally show preferences for environmental color. Domestic turkeys, for example preferred supplementary ultraviolet light in their habitat. Rhesus monkeys and domestic chickens showed an aversion to habitats lit by red lamps. The interiors of two barns at a horse farm were respectively painted red and blue. The blue barn had fewer flies. Horses housed in it cooled out faster from their workouts and were calmer. Horses housed in the red barn took longer to cool down and were emotionally "hotter." Humans are affected by environmental color. Red light increased the severity of motor disorders, interfered with thinking and problem solving, increased anxiety, and provoked negative mood states (Note that many restaurants use red color schemes; think about the effect on our digestion!). Exposure to blue-green reversed these effects. Rhesus monkeys became more alert in red light compared with blue, and scanned the environment more. Mice showed a clear and consistent individual preference for white cage color, followed by black or green. The least preferred color was red, and mice who lived in red cages were more anxious. Some colors such as red and yellow are effective warning signals, and may be seen on venomous species such as coral snakes.

To my knowledge there are no studies that indicate how dogs react to environmental color, however, I'd assume they do react, and probably in the same ways as other organisms with similar sensory capabilities. The ability to see the color is not important; even blind people can perceive differences in colors, and some people can "see" colors with their fingers. Colors have electromagnetic frequencies, and it is the effects of these that result in observable changes in mood and behavior. Since a state of anxiety is conducive neither to learning nor to maintaining stable relationships, how might you change the color of your environment to promote balance? Pink, peach, blue-green and lavender are some of my favorites.

What words do you use to speak to your dog? We're well-acquainted with the effects thunderstorms and firecrackers have on our dogs. But what about human language? Harsh, loud, derogatory language disrupts emotions and behavior. The vibration of positive words has the power to produce positive emotions and behavior. This is why I suggest that having dogs listen to talk radio or TV while clients are away might not be a good idea. The words that are spoken as well as the vibrational rate of the speech affect our dogs' emotions and behavior. Ethologist Patricia McConnell has studied the effects of the human voice on animal behavior extensively, finding that low, slow, descending tones tend to decrease motor activity, and high-pitched, fast, ascending tones tend to increase it.

And think about the power of a name. Veterinary behaviorist Karen Overall refers to this when she states that if she had a Rottweiler she would name it Fluffy to diffuse the negativity associated with the Rottweiler image. Regrettably I've gotten into trouble with this last one. I got a call from a woman with a Pit Bull who had bitten several people. The dog's name was Rambo. I suggested that until our appointment she might consider the implications of the dog's name and potentially change it. Her terse response was, "I suppose you'd like me to change him into a spaniel while I'm at it!" She canceled her appointment.

I've spent a lot of time writing about environmental concerns, because the environment, both within and outside the animal, is responsible for shaping emotions which in turn generate behavior. I think many of our animals are on sensory overload most of the time, and this establishes a potential for the development of issues. I'm convinced that the only thing keeping my family from chaos during Kiwi's convalescence from cancer and chemotherapy was the calm, peaceful environment I provided my other three dogs when I didn't have time to get them the exercise they needed. When I create a treatment plan for a client, I first try to eliminate anything in the environment that could cause or contribute to an emotional state that may generate a behavior problem. As a result, I often find the actual inappropriate behaviors disappear or are much diminished and easier to resolve.

We are only beginning to understand and appreciate the intricacy and uniqueness of the sensory abilities of non-human animals. It is appropriate to accommodate their different sensory needs as part of the practice of relationship.

Intent

What exactly is intent? What is its significance in the practice of *eros*? The Vedic traditions of India describe intent as a force of nature. Nothing in the universe happens without intent. We form intentions from the desire to satisfy needs. Needs may be satisfied in many ways. The purest need, with the greatest potential for satisfaction through intent, is the need which derives from relationship with and service to others. Physician and author Deepak Chopra writes, "Intention orchestrates infinite possibilities." Thus with our dogs and other companion animals, as we seek to satisfy our need for them to behave appropriately, we must also address the question, "What's in it for them if they do?" and I don't mean cookies and tennis balls. Right intent must also orchestrate the satisfaction of our animals' needs for engagement, relationship, order and stability in ways that are meaningful and fulfilling to them.

The tools of intent are connections. Connections with each other, with the natural world, with past and future, with the universe. All things created are related. Our dogs seek connection with us in many wonderful ways. One of these may be telepathy, which, according to biologist Rupert Sheldrake, is enabled by the presence of morphogenetic fields.

These fields may be defined by the principles of quantum physics. Sheldrake's work focuses on self-organizing systems contained within morphogenetic fields, regions of influence in space-time located in and around the systems they organize. The fields help organize perception, behavior, cognition, emotion, and perhaps even spirituality. We and our animal companions form social systems organized by morphogenetic fields. The structure of our field is determined by its history, which creates a kind of cumulative memory formed by self-resonance with a morphogenetic unit's own past and by resonance with all previous similar systems. This pool of memory determines the organization of new fields. Thus there is pooled memory for *Canis familiaris*, the domestic dog, and for *Homo sapiens*, modern humans. There is also, then, a pooled memory for the morphogenetic field that organizes the symbiotic relationship between these two species. As historical patterns organized by the field are repeated, their probability for repetition increases and they become habitual.

Sheldrake proposes that there is a starting point for any given field, caused by what he describes as a "creative jump." Could the starting point for the human-canine bond have been one of these "creative jumps," initiating some 100,000 years ago the morphogenetic fields we supposedly inhabit with our dogs? Other events which support the "creative jump" hypothesis may include the population of horses in the United States spontaneously losing their fear of cars and locomotives in the early 20th century, and gaps in the evolutionary line of species, the so-called "missing links." Since members of social groups, that is, we and our dogs, are members of the same, morphogenetically organized social system, we are interlinked through our minds and senses and interact continually, *whether we realize it or not!*

Here is yet another reason to increase our mindfulness toward our animals: to guide the interlinkage and interactions toward habit/expectation paradigms that become a positive guiding force not only for our system in the present, but also to provide the memory of positive interactions which will guide the formation of all systems that derive through time from our present one. Even when we are separated from our dogs, it appears we may retain a connection that may explain such phenomena as dogs "knowing" when we're on our way home, or our sensing over a distance that something may be amiss with our animal. Since we are linked with objects of perception (that is, our dogs) through these morphogenetic fields, according to Sheldrake we are able to affect them with our intention and attention. Have you ever had the feeling that someone was staring at you, even though your back was turned? Research has determined that this is an actual rather than imagined phenomenon.

An invisible cord, likened to an elastic band, connects us with our dogs. Through this cord, communication can occur. Dogs seem to read our minds beyond what cues from our body language would enable. Thus it becomes important to synchronize our intent with what we desire to communicate to our animals. It is, for example, effective to not only cue a recall by calling, "Over here!" and getting my pup to chase me, but also to send to the pup the image of a chunk of cheese being devoured off my outstretched hand as she arrives in front of me. British dog trainer Barbara Woodhouse stressed the importance of synchronizing thoughts, words and actions during training to prevent the dog telepathically receiving the wrong message. Woodhouse expressed with frustration the difficulty of teaching classes when dogs responded to her intent, by lying down, for example, before she could voice her instructions to the owners to cue their dogs into a down.

The practice of *eros* requires intent with its accompanying behaviors to be whole and complete; it cannot be halfhearted if the correct path toward the desired outcome is to be established.

In *Kinship With All Life*, J. Allen Boone relates an experience communicating with Strongheart. Deciding to interview the dog, Boone mentally asked him a number of questions, then relaxed and cleared his mind. To his amazement he received detailed answers to nearly every question he had posed, and was able to verify the answers with other sources. Boone described the language of telepathy as universal and ancient, one which enables every life form to communicate with every other life form, provided hearts and minds are open to the possibilities.

Regrettably the power of intent, along with telepathy, clairvoyance and other forms of non-ordinary perception, has been discounted by Western cultures. These phenomena are validated, however, by non-Western cultures, and are part of our collective unconscious. This means that we still have access to these methods if we wish to revive and develop our ability to use them. In her book *Mutant Message Down Under*, Marlo Morgan described her experience with silent communication while living among an Aboriginal group in Australia. She noticed that during the group's nomadic wanderings they seldom vocalized to each other, and she was astonished at the realization that, during the silence, a tremendous amount of communication was occurring telepathically, even though some members of the group might be miles apart.

The following may have also been a telepathic experience.

I noticed Diamond carrying her ball on the left side of her mouth. She had damaged her upper right canine and needed a root canal. Three weeks after the procedure, she came into the room where I was working, carrying her ball. Thinking she wanted to play, I started talking to her in a playful, teasing tone. In response to my attempt to engage her, she turned and left the room. This was repeated several times. Play was apparently not her intent.

> *A thought came into my head: it's not about play, it's about the tooth. I'm using my whole mouth to carry the ball. An instant after this realization occurred to me, she left the room and laid down.*

Another interesting event occurred while I was helping a client learn to use the Tellington Method with her cat.

> *I asked if I might demonstrate the technique on her cat, with the caveat that the cat would need to accept my touch. I approached the cat and silently thought, "May I touch you?" Before I had a chance to finish the thought I heard a shouted "NO!" I asked again, "Do you mind if I touch you?" Again, before the thought was completely out of my mind, came a shouted "YES!" I told the client what I'd just experienced. She said the cat was often aversive to any touch from strangers and was quite accepting of her cat's apparent communication of this fact.*

If you take time to reflect, you'll probably find you've had similar experiences as described above. Even if one doesn't believe in telepathy, might it be possible to do a better job of communicating with our animals if we consciously set our intent, visualizing our expectation in our mind, as we cue behaviors with body and voice. The beauty of intent, of course, is that it can be done any time and any place. Our dogs don't need to see us in order to pick up this kind of signal. I suppose it requires a leap of faith on our part that they will indeed receive our telepathic signals of intent, but given the impoverished nature of some of our interactions with our animals I think it's definitely worth trying. "Can't hurt, might help," Tellington Method practitioners are often heard to say. I would like to see us recognize and become more mindful of the embryonic non-ordinary perceptions I believe we possess, and incorporate their development into our relationships with our dogs.

Intentions represent seeds planted in our consciousness, and even our spirit. The power of intent is that it contains within itself the means for its fulfillment. We are able to effect change in our environment through our fears and desires: our intentions. So it behooves us to be mindful of what we feel and wish for.

Humor

Practice is hard work, and work which we should take most seriously. But it's essential that we have a break now and then, because unending seriousness seriously unbalances a system. Humor can provide a welcome respite.

Laughter uplifts us. According to the Koran, "He deserves paradise who makes his companions laugh." Our dogs, then, are deserving of paradise! So many times their antics are humorous. Picture a massive Golden Retriever, weighing over 100 pounds, being towed out of our pond by his tail, the hair of which was clenched in the teeth of a mischievous one-year-old, over-achieving Labrador. Or imagine the delight of watching my ten-week-old Tom leaping into the air to chase swallows flying near to the ground. Often the more spontaneous and outrageous an event, the greater the probability that some humorous outcome will occur. The stronger the emotions that are in play, the more intense the laughter will be.

Laughter and humor make us less defensive and open up communication channels, helping to increase the cohesion among members of a group. Just like people, dogs learn most effectively if they're having fun. This means we need to keep the environment positive and upbeat. Laughter helps us do that. When the dogs feel our happy mood, they enjoy being close to us. Humor, with its accompanying happiness and laughter, is like a dog magnet. Our dogs are teachers in the realm of humor. They seldom appear embarrassed. They show their feelings spontaneously, and are always delighted to share positive experiences with us. Some dogs have even been seen to smile in response to humorous or disarming situations. Those who can laugh together also share a level of trust, which is essential for a balanced relationship.

We can take a proactive approach to humor by anticipating stressful situations and visualizing humorous responses as alternatives to negative reactions.

I know Kiwi is inclined to wander off. A pattern has emerged such that I can predict the point in our walk at which he's most likely to stray. As we approach the house, our trail forks: left to the house, right to the road and adventure. He waits just before the fork while I go ahead. As I'm letting the other dogs into the house, my attention is diverted and that's when he makes a break for it. But he's not particularly quick. Twice now I've chased up the right fork, surprising him with a sudden, loud "HAH!" just as he's about to disappear over the crest of the hill. "HAH!" turns into silly cackling at his look of surprise and my delight at catching him in the act. He sheepishly turns himself around, runs to catch up as I backpedal away from him, and gets hugs and kisses when he catches me.

Acceptance

Within our human perceptions, things have limits. Limits define for our understanding all sorts of things, including an individual's capacity for change. This capacity is determined by a number of criteria, such as the quality of life experiences and genetic heritage. Some of us have greater capacity to change and develop than others. Some animals, both human and non-human, have greater capacity to relate than others. The facilitator for relationship is respect. Respect capacity. If we demand more of a dog than she is truly capable of, we strain capacity. The resultant fallout may be a behavior problem that erodes the relationship. A wonderful expression of acceptance is the Serenity Prayer:

> God, grant me the Serenity to accept the things I cannot change, the Courage to change things that I can, and the Wisdom to know the difference.

It's so important to accept the other as she is, with all her limitations. As we accept our dogs with their limitations, we must also accept ourselves with our limitations. Acceptance helps us disengage when we are unable to carry a relationship beyond a certain point without fatally unbalancing it.

Limits are implicit in approval. It's important to not confuse acceptance with approval. Unconditional approval is impossible because limits, by their nature, are conditional. We cannot approve of something unless it falls within predefined limits. Do our dogs, whom we've already decided are deserving of paradise, need to fall within certain limits to be accepted and acceptable? Are we closing ourselves and our dogs off from reaching our full potential by placing too much emphasis on approval rather than acceptance? Are we setting up obstacles to engagement, relationship, order and stability by insistence on approved standards? Dogs don't care about approval, judgments, standards or deviations. Dogs just want to have fun! They care only for what gives them the best feeling and greatest chance of survival at any given moment.

Sometimes that even involves altruistic behaviors that cause them to sacrifice their lives for us, or just the opportunity to admire and respect those they live with. They take what's given to them and deal with it, though suffering may be involved. They generally don't ask questions or complain. Mostly they seem to accept us as we are, even though we may not satisfy their basic needs for food, shelter, safety, belonging and recognition. I qualify the preceding statement with "mostly," because an incident occurred which causes me to think that our dogs are not always so accepting and do have ways of showing it.

My first dog, Molly, and I spent much of our free time exploring the woods and rivers of northern Wisconsin. Usually we had a great time, but one particular trip was memorable for its hardship. We were canoeing down a remote river. It had been a rainy, humid weekend, with clouds of mosquitoes. We weren't enjoying the trip, and my plan was to make camp early, get a good sleep and start for home in the morning. We were wet, tired, and covered in layers of insect repellant, sweat and sand. I beached the canoe on a sandbar in the middle of the river, where the mosquitoes were less intense, intending to have a bath in the river so I could rest more comfortably. Molly was likewise needing attention, and let me know it by repeated attempts to rub up against the towel I was trying to get out of my pack. I reasoned I could better meet her needs if I took care of mine first, so I gently pushed her out of my way. With furrowed brow that seemed to communicate disgust, she backed up and looked me straight in the eye. She turned, walked 20 feet or so upriver, and laid down in the middle of it with her back to me. She refused to come when I was ready to clean her up; I had to go get her. I'm sure she was feeling as miserable as I was, and saw no reason to wait her turn.

In terms of unconditional love and acceptance of our behavior, do dogs really have a choice?

Acceptance constitutes a covenant. Ethologist Konrad Lorenz reflects on the ancient covenant between man and dog that was "signed voluntarily and without obligation by each of the contracting parties." In its voluntariness this covenant is unique among species of domesticated animals. While on the surface it may be described as opportunistic, is this covenant in its deeper recesses an intuitive leap of faith that the potential relationship between man and dog is of a divine nature?

* *

Practicing the Concepts in Chapter 1

1. Keeping a Journal

    Despite our emotional, reactive, self-interested and opportunistic tendencies, we can choose to behave in other ways. Reinforce this choice by keeping a daily journal of your emotional experiences. A simple lined notebook works well. On the left-hand page, write down a detailed account of events as you remember them. On the right-hand page, write how it made you feel, why, and what you did to release or embrace an emotion. Write about happy experiences as well as sad ones. This is a lot like writing down all the food you eat to plan a weight loss program, except in more detail. The journal increases mindfulness, making a proactive approach possible. You may find that with the reflections and insights your journal offers you, emotions like fear and anger may not take as long to go away, may not be as strong, or may even stop altogether. Emotions like happiness, joy and anticipation may become more frequent or last longer. In my studies toward my doctorate, the best advice anyone ever gave me was to write something every day about what I had read, or an experience I'd had. The capacity of writing to make thoughts visual allows us to think in new and different ways.

2. Choosing Approaches

    Record your proactive and reactive approaches to two of your dog's problem behaviors in the figure on the following page.
    -   Note the behaviors generated by the feelings in each approach.
    -   Think about which approach is more useful, and how each might affect the relationship between you and your dog.
    Refer to page 10 for additional insights on proactive vs. reactive approaches.

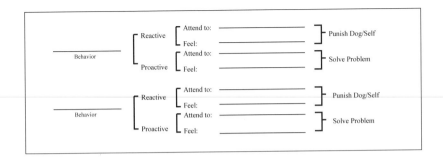

Practicing the Concepts in Chapter 2

1. Checking In

   What a dog sees is what a dog pays attention to. What a dog attends to is what a dog engages with. Create engagement with your dog by reinforcing spontaneous eye contact. Each time your dog takes the initiative to look at you, mark the behavior by saying the word "Yes!" followed by a reward of lavish praise and food or play. Most dogs will start to check in with you more frequently. If you have the eyes, you have the dog!

2. Savor the Aroma

   Some may not appreciate this exercise, but I find it fascinating. Dogs are probably more into smelly things than any other kind of stimulus, and much dog communication is based on the perception and interpretation of chemicals in urine, feces, anal secretions, and scent glands. Dogs have some interesting scents about them that I was intrigued to investigate. One of my favorites is the pads of their feet. Puppy breath is another. While investigating my dog's pads, I discovered that the scent is strongest in the morning, while they are lying in bed with me. They have a nutty, sweet odor that I love. I also found that the scent is slightly different for each dog. So for those of you who are likewise fascinated, engage with your dog at an uncommon level: sniff and savor the odor of his footpads.

3. Play

Researchers in the United Kingdom found that dogs responded preferentially to human signals initiating play with them. Dogs engaged in play 100% of the time when humans did the following:

- Bent forward and downward until the torso was horizontal and level with the waist.
- Moved quickly towards or away from the dog in a chase game.
- Shuffled feet, quick, short lunge toward dog, bowed forward.

Signals such as simulating a dog's play bow were also effective 75-90% of the time. The researchers also found that inviting the dog to play in a high-pitched voice enhanced the value of the visual signals. Three times each day, initiate a play session with your dog by doing one or more of these actions while you verbally invite your dog to play in a happy, teasing voice. Play sessions need not be longer than two or three minutes, unless, of course, you and your dog want to! Keep a journal of your dog's responses. At the end of three weeks, assess whether you've increased the amount of engagement you and your dog have with each other. I like to use a scale from 1-10, with "1" being the worst and "10" being the best.

4. Two Hearts Visualization.

This is the visualization with which I begin my Tellington Method workshops. It helps us set our intent for the work ahead of us.

Make a calm, quiet space for you and your dog, where you will not be disturbed for at least 10 minutes. Sit or lay quietly next to each other. Close your eyes. See in your heart of hearts a pinpoint of dazzling golden light. Imagine this point expanding to fill your whole heart until your heart disappears in the brilliant aura. Imagine a golden filament traveling from your heartlight to a point of dazzling golden light within your dog's heart. As the filament makes contact, the pinpoint of light within your dog's heart begins to expand, filling his entire heart with warm, loving golden light. This light comes back to you through the filament. As you sit with your dog, sharing your heart light, imagine the two of you surrounded by a bubble of rosy light, the light of love. Share with your dog thoughts or feelings of forgiveness for past mistakes, hopes and dreams for the future, peaceful intent, or anything else you consider important for her to receive. Open your heart and mind to receive back from her anything she may send.

5. Pono/Pilikia

    This is a Hawaiian philosophy adapted by Linda Tellington-Jones to help you better understand your relationship with your animal. *Pono* is excellence, an ideal state of being, while *Pilikia* means drama or trauma. When our dog has an issue, for example, aggression (*pilikia*), it's easy to allow the issue to overshadow what we love (*pono*) about this animal.

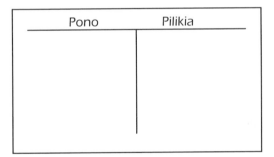

Pono	Pilikia

- Draw the above diagram on a sheet of paper.
- Under pono, write down everything you love and appreciate about your dog.
- Under pilikia, write down all of the issues you have with your dog.
- Compare both sides. Have you gained any insights which may lead to a resolution of the issues you're facing?

Practicing the Concepts in Chapter 3

1. Determining Needs

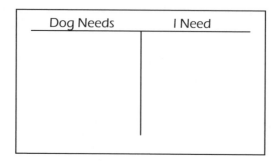

Dog Needs	I Need

- Draw the above diagram on a sheet of paper.
- Record as many needs as you can think of, no matter how insignificant they may seem.
- Reflect on how well all needs are being met.
- If there are a large number of needs for either or both of you, how can you manage the environment to satisfy more needs?

Practicing the Concepts in Chapter 4

1. Implement a learn-to-earn program if you haven't already done so.

Practicing the Concepts in Chapter 5

1. Take Care of Yourself

    Maintaining a stable relationship with your dog depends to a great degree on your continuing guidance and direction, something you're unable to provide if you're unwell. When an emergency occurs on an airplane, oxygen masks are released. Flight attendants emphasize the need to put on your own oxygen mask before you tend to the needs of children or others who may need your help. The same is true here. If something happens to you, who will care for your dog? Make an effort to assess your lifestyle. Are your habits conducive to the health and well-being which will allow you to be able to meet your dog's needs?

2.   Repairing Broken Bonds

In normal adult-infant human play, adults pace invitations to play corresponding with their babies' readiness to respond. Infants express behaviors such as smiling, looking, and cooing to match the adults' invitations. This is called "synchrony." Averted eyes, stiffening or abrupt change in posture, or unhappy noises indicate lack of synchrony. Adults can disrupt or prevent synchrony by ignoring the infant's invitation to interact, or overstimulating a tired baby.   Repeatedly ignoring infants who make play overtures causes them to put less effort into responding. And infants whose caregivers are intrusive and overstimulating defend themselves by turning away, crying inconsolably or going to sleep. Synchrony can be achieved with non-human species as well. Think of this as a "dance" where your dog leads.

Watch for signals that your dog is stressed, such as licking the lips, yawning, averting the eyes and head, or walking away. When you see your dog do any of these things, assess the situation and decide what can be changed to remove the stressors. This may be as simple as turning sideways to the dog rather than making a frontal approach. What does your dog do in response to the change you have made? Make it a practice to watch your dog carefully for these behaviors that signal stress. Turid Rugaas' book *On Talking Terms With Dogs* is an excellent reference to help you tune in to your dog's signaling.

Practicing the Concepts in Chapter 6

1.   Breathing, Self

Breathing is a powerful technique for self-engagement, helping us to focus on our emotions and perceptions. Slow, rhythmic, deep breathing helps release stress and stuck energy which can create negative emotions. These, in turn, can result in disorganized and ineffective thoughts and behaviors.

Arrange a calm, quiet and comfortable place in which to lie down for five to ten minutes. Close your eyes. Breathe in slowly through your nose to the count of four, filling your lungs from the bottom, your diaphragm, to the top. Hold that breath for four seconds. Then exhale to the count of four. Refrain from breathing for four seconds: the still point. As you inhale, imagine the incoming air as a cloud of light moving through your body and filling every organ and cell with light.

2.   Breathing, Other

Breathing together with your dog can help you focus and become calm and centered. While your dog is lying relaxed on her side, and you're in your calm, quiet, comfortable place, watch her abdomen and synchronize your breathing with hers. It's a wonderful opportunity to become more mindful of the present, and increase your connection. It enhances the effect if you sit next to her and put your hand on her rib cage, feeling it rise and fall.

3.   Morphogenetic Fields

Spend 5-10 minutes in a room with your animal, basically just hanging out together. Allow your animal to come and go freely. Imagine that you have a bubble around yourself. Your dog also has a bubble. Imagine these two bubbles connected by an elastic band. Visualize the band extending and retracting between you as your dog moves to various places around the room. If your dog moves out of sight, imagine the elastic band continuing to connect your bubbles.

4.   "Look" with Your Hands

How do you typically touch your dog? Do you rough up his fur with short, fast, back and forth strokes? Do you pat or thump? Do you hit? Most of these are mindless and reactive. At the very least, these types of touches tend to stimulate arousal. At worst they create anxiety, fear and pain. Practice a different way of relating.

Place your hand lightly on your dog's body. Begin to move your hand very slowly, allowing it to be limp so that it conforms to the contours of your dog. Touch every part of your dog in this way, slowly and mindfully moving your hand, and paying attention to any sensations, such as warmth or coldness in any places, softness or rigidity in the muscles, quality of coat and skin, etc. Especially attend to any areas where your dog is reluctant to be touched. What might this tell you, and how is the information useful?

5. Shared Glances

Practice holding warm and loving eye contact with your dog. Allow your eyelids to droop so your eyes become squinty, but keep them soft and relaxed. Does your dog evade even the softest eye contact? What might this tell you?

6. Meaning Without Words

If you stop listening to your words, and listen instead to the tone of your voice, what message does your voice send? Is it anger? Joy? Enthusiasm? Do you tend to speak faster, louder, and at a higher pitch in intense emotional states? When your voice goes slow, low and soft, are you feeling bored, depressed or content? When you become silent, are you focused on committing some act of aggression, or are you contemplative or maybe even sleeping?

Watch your dog for her reactions to different tones in your voice. Record her responses in your journal to increase your awareness of the effect your voice has on his behavior.

7. Cultivating a Sense of Humor with Your Dog

    List in your journal the things your dog does that make you laugh. List three things you do with your dog that are fun for both of you. List three things your dog has taught you about not taking life too seriously.

8. Teaching Never Ends

    Dogs only stop learning when we stop teaching. Just as older humans can keep their minds sharp by doing a crossword puzzle or reading the newspaper every day, even very old dogs are capable of learning. Spend ten minutes each day with your dog, teaching something new. An easy way to do this is to simply get a clicker and click and reward every novel behavior your dog does, or use the word "yes" in place of the click. This can create an incredible degree of engagement when dogs begin to experiment to see what will earn them a click or a yes.

                  *

Reflections . . .

1. If we practice we will get better.
2. Mindful touch is informative and empowering.
3. Bodywork allows us to access emotions at the cellular level.
4. Emotions motivate behavior.
5. Body position influences emotions.
6. Quality of the environment determines quality of behavior.
7. We all exist in interrelated systems.
8. Intentions can become self-fulfilling prophecies.
9. Laugh.
10. Seek acceptance rather than approval.

The Power of the World works in Circles.

— *Black Elk*

7   *Transcendence*

transcendence \tran(t)s-'en-dən(t)s\   1b. extending or lying beyond the limits of ordinary experience.

facilitated by: faith

What is Dog?

Cultures past and present around the world relate to Dog symbolically and mythologically. In the early Christian faith, Dog represented guardianship and symbolized the priestly role. In India, Dog is a metaphor for all caste systems, and represents the small becoming great. Thus Dog is a metaphor for the entire human race.   In some Native American cultures Dog is a symbol of motherhood and nurturing. The Lakota Indians believe that eating a dog in the *yuwipi* ceremony bestows many blessings. In dogs we see qualities that we ourselves admire and aspire to, such as faithfulness and protection. Many of the jobs dogs perform involve some type of protective role to which we humans like to attribute a quality of faithfulness, such as service dog, sniffer dog, companion dog, and guard dog.

Dog is not a Human. We do them a grave injustice by treating them as such.   Nevertheless, I believe dogs are entitled to many of the same rights that a human is entitled to, as well as some which we are not. Dogs pant foul breath on us and scent the air with intestinal gas, often with impunity and occasionally with our amusement. They have the right to behave this way because they have no control over these expressions, just as a young child has no control over its elimination needs. We are both animals with species-specific animal needs. The great diversity of life on our planet exists because the environment has been able to meet the needs of uncountable individual species for eons. When needs can no longer be met, species become extinct.

If I were a dog, my deepest desire would be to be treated like a dog, which means all my doggie needs would be satisfied. If I wish to eat poop, allow me to do so. I enjoy the taste. If I wish to roll in the carcass of a dead fish, allow me to do so; I enjoy the smell. If I wish to run, allow me to do so; it is my connection with the earth and who I am. I only ask that in the world you have created, in which I must live, allow me to do these things, which I need and enjoy, in safety. Indulge me with caring and safety, and I will be at your side till death, and perhaps beyond.

As we connect with our animals at a cellular, molecular or perhaps even energetic and spiritual level, it becomes possible to transcend the limits of our human experience. The universe can be conceptualized as a network of interacting particles and waves, with linkages that bind individual particles into a single quantum system. Within this system exists a consciousness. It is increasingly recognized and accepted that non-human animals, as well as plants and inanimate objects, have a consciousness. Connecting to this consciousness allows us to discover insights and perspectives far beyond the consciousness of our human form. Shamanic practitioners are noted for their ability to assume the shapes and behaviors of other species. According to psychologist Carl Jung, the vast "collective unconscious" makes such experiences not only possible, but eminently achievable by nearly everyone. Psychologist Stanislav Grof writes of how each of us is a holographic image of the universe, of everything that exists, has existed and will exist. As such we potentially have access, in an experiential way, to the entire network of the cosmos. Thus it is theoretically possible for us to move among spatial and chronological dimensions, transcending the limits of our physical forms. Wishing can indeed make it so!

I find it extremely reassuring to not only believe in this connection with something larger than myself, but also to believe that my beloved dogs are a part of it as well. Actually, it goes far beyond connection. Probably a better word to describe the feeling would be integration, providing a wondrously safe and secure sense of belonging to a cosmic creation of infinite possibilities. This becomes even more gratifying when I realize that I share this connection and integration with my animal companions, and helps me feel a profound sense of responsibility to insure that my actions toward them are positive, because what I do to them I also do to myself.

The work of Sheldrake and others seems to indicate that our social systems will evolve beyond our ancestral habits with increasing speed. Learning new skills can become progressively easier. With respect to teaching our dogs, witness the technical developments in equipment in just the past twenty years. We are no longer bound to use a collar around an animal's neck. Innovations such as head collars and harnesses which attach the leash to a point on the chest are changing the way we mechanically guide our dog's movements.

Sheldrake argues that connections across time and space create the form, development, and behavior of organisms in the phenomenon he describes as morphogenetic fields. These fields, which are not directly measurable with the tools currently available to us, have cumulative effects which, over time, may account for the apparently spontaneous development of behaviors in organisms that have no direct connection with the initiator of the behavior. Thus dogs seem to know and respond to the distant whereabouts of their humans at a given time of day, waiting at the door for their person's arrival, even though the arrival may happen at random times. Horses avoid barbed wire fences, and archeologists pursue missing links which may never be found because they do not exist. So on what journeys might engagement with our dog or other companion animals lead us? The mind boggles at the possibilities! Some scientists have even postulated that if one part of the universe (humans) is obviously conscious, and all parts of the universe are integrated and unified, all of the universe is conscious. I find this very reassuring, especially considering that if this "cosmic web" is integrated and indivisible, we've got a terrific support system and can't possibly fail!

It also becomes abundantly clear that, within the connections of the cosmic web, whatever we do to others, down to the smallest grain of sand, we do to ourselves. Do we play a part in creating our animal's issues? We absolutely do. Whether the part we play is deliberate or out of ignorance, to reach a state of transcendence we need to acknowledge and accept our role. Thus, take charge of your animal. His well-being, and yours, depend upon it. Have expectations. Set boundaries. By starting with known limits, the known becomes limitless.

The fact that you've reached the end of this book shows you are curious about changing the relationship you share with your dog, and maybe even want to do it, and you can, if you so choose.

My Wish For You and Your Dog: Interspecies Synergy

To me, dogs are spiritual beings. So are all beings, for that matter. But from my individual perspective, dogs are unique because of the connection we have forged with them over millennia, a connection we share with no other. Consider the Lakota legend of how dogs came to be with us:

> One day the Creator looked down from Above and noticed that all the Humans and Four-Leggeds were getting into a lot of trouble. At that time, all Beings spoke the same language. Creator got so angry at the lack of Harmony that he decided to punish everyone. So he caused all Beings to speak different languages. To make certain these conflicts never occurred again, he also began to split the Earth between the Humans and Four-Leggeds. The chasm widened till it was almost impossible for anyone to jump across to the other side. But at the last

minute, Dog jumped from the Four-Leggeds' side to the Humans' side of the chasm. From that moment on, Dog stood with Man. (Source Unknown)

Humanistic psychologist Anthony Sutich coined the term "interspecies synergy" to describe the transpersonal experience that all of us are capable of having with others, including our dogs and companion animals. Through such mystical and creative processes we more closely achieve that potential perfection of which we are all capable. Through engagement, relationship, order, stability and practice, we can achieve with our dogs that sweet sense of interspecies synergy, and together will be more than we could ever be alone. This is *eros*, the love instinct striving for union and the creation of higher units. Thus begins the process of transcendence!

Disengagement

Sometimes it is necessary to disengage from a relationship. The nature of the disengagement, including how and if it is successfully negotiated by the individuals undergoing it, may determine whether the process of disengagement causes that relationship to take on a transcendent quality. Upon reading Jeffrey Masson's *When Elephants Weep*, I had cause to ponder whether dogs really are able to transfer affections readily from one home to the next as some believe. I've heard a number of behaviorists and trainers say that they do, but I'm not so sure. It seems to me that a lot of behavior problems have their roots in the trauma of losing one's home. When social beings are uprooted from all they find familiar, is it reasonable to think they will carry on behaving normally? Does this kind of forced disengagement really have no effect? Author Elizabeth Marshall Thomas describes how her Husky, Maria, reacted to the loss of the dog Misha, with whom she had bonded. After Misha was returned to his previous home, Maria stationed herself in the window from which she had watched him depart. After a number of weeks elapsed, she apparently realized the separation was permanent. Depression set in. She never recovered from the loss, and other male dogs failed to interest her.

When I see animals in my practice that seem spiritless, joyless, confused or depressed, I can't help but wonder what traumatic disengagement they've suffered in their lives. Do they, indeed, transfer their affections as easily as we imagine? There is a widely held belief that dogs are a rather promiscuous species, that bonding is important only in the moment. Thomas' anecdote would seem to indicate the opposite; that dogs, like humans, form lasting pair bonds and grieve the loss of a partner. It's only our husbandry practices that perpetuate the belief in promiscuity, as we arrange marriages of convenience for our dogs, based on the most economically profitable outcome, without regard for the animals' perspectives on the subject. In these practices it would appear we are very much disengaged from both their needs and their feelings.

There is another kind of disengagement, a rather more permanent kind.

February 22, 2006:

I struggle with the news that Kiwi has cancer. The cytologist's report commented, "The lymphosarcoma is of high grade malignancy." By my best guess, Kiwi is 17 years old. Do I let this dog go? Do I try to keep him here awhile longer, knowing the expense and rigor of treatment? I watched him this morning, running with the other dogs, as fast as his aged bones would allow. But running, nonetheless. Responding to play overtures from Diamond with his characteristic disgust, passing the refrigerator test with flying colors...

Do I try to keep him here awhile longer? Do I let him go? Addressing such questions is also part of the practice of *eros*, because at some point, we all need to disengage from the relationship we share with our dogs in this material world.

A Mindful Dog, Teaching

Certain events stop us in our tracks, changing the direction of our lives forever.

July 22, 2006:

Tom seemed out of sorts, refusing to go outside, retreating to the laundry room. He'd been like this before, always recovering his usual cheerful attitude in a day or so. At bedtime he went as usual to his corner behind the bed; he seemed to like curling himself into a corner. His sleep that night was punctuated by what sounded like brief attempts to clear his stomach of some irritation.

July 23, 2006:

He refused to go outside in the morning. Indeed, he could barely walk. I took his temperature: 104. I called the university to advise them we were on our way. I carried him into the exam room. Test results showed elevated kidney values. He was admitted. Thinking this was like all the other times where he ultimately rebounded, I drove home to await news. The student called me that evening; Tom had developed vomiting and diarrhea, with neurological changes. She was concerned. They would call me first thing in the morning.

July 24, 2006:

8am. The doctor called to say Tom had taken a turn for the worse. Should they attempt to resuscitate? I cancelled my clients, quickly dressed. and drove to the hospital. The doctor explained the situation saying Tom had arrested at 10.15; they had resuscitated per my instructions. As we talked, tears streaming down my face, my sobs muffled in a handkerchief, her pager advised Tom had had another episode of erratic heart rhythm. "Please, may I see my dog," I pleaded.

"He probably won't recognize you," she said. She led me through a blur of people and corridors to the room where Tom lay. My first sight of him caused me to catch my breath. My beloved Tom, virtually unconscious, hooked to a cardiac monitor and an endotrachial tube, his exquisite flag of a tail bound up in a blue bandage to prevent soiling, his eyes dull and glazed. His breathing was almost imperceptible. I placed my hand over his heart, telling him how much I loved him. He drew a breath. I felt his heart rhythm change, and then stop.

The vet techs placed him tenderly in a small white box, arranging a white blanket around him. In a state of unreality I led them to my car where they gently placed the box on the floor for the ride home.

In our garden we took him from the box, laying his body on the green earth one last time. We held a ceremony for him, to ask blessings for his safe journey. Then I lay down next to him. For hours I cradled him, cried over him, and talked to him. The bits of my shattered heart, soul and spirit dissipated like smoke in the wind.

For four days I ate almost nothing. No food could feed my hunger for his physical presence; the feel of his coat, the light in his smoky brown eyes. I had thought that losing my father was the hardest experience I would ever have. I was wrong. Never in my life have I experienced the anguish that accompanied Tom's passing. Nothing could have prepared me for the suddenness and tragedy of the event.

In the days following, I found my physical, mental and emotional processes disrupted. I'd start a task only to forget moments later how to complete it. I'd find myself in another room of the house or office and not know how or why I was there. I, whoever or whatever I was, had checked out, disconnected from ordinary reality.

Who can make sense of such a loss? How can it in any way contribute to one's personal process in a positive way? Just as **eros** has two sides, so also do tragedies potentially reveal the light hidden in their darkness. While introspection is important, a dangerous tendency is for us to withdraw into ourselves in the face of tragedy, limiting its potential to reveal its light. We thus may fail to transcend its darkness, and become sucked into it. With the support of my friends and colleagues, animal communicator Carol Schultz and shamanic practitioner Mary Baumstark, I began to find my way through this dark night of the soul. Assuring me that Tom's spirit was safe, they affirmed his role as companion, guide and teacher. Healing had begun.

Just as we take care to teach our dogs mindfully, we must take equal care to be mindful of our dogs' teachings. Reflections on Tom's life with me, his last hours, and the role I played in his journey on this plane delivered powerful, highly-charged insights, often accompanied by floods of tears. A particularly intense event occurred the day after his passing.

> *Still in a state of non-ordinary reality, I was compelled to take a walk along the tree line across from our house. I called and searched for Tom. I sat down on the edge of a meadow. An image of him appeared in my mind, a clear barrier between us. "Listen to the South Wind. I am there. Look for me and I will find you. I'm coming back to you."*

Images of small, brown Cocker spaniels began appearing daily and unexpectedly in many different places: on the event calendar at the bookstore, a sympathy card sent by our vet, an artist's rendering in stained glass in the vendor booth adjacent to mine at a dog show, a book cover glimpsed in a shop window. Were these messages from Tom? I choose to think they were. Sheldrake argues that morphogenetic fields extend through time and space; why not into non-ordinary realities? It gives me great comfort to believe, with all my heart, that somewhere out there is a little, brown, scruffy, spindle-legged pup with a runny nose and an attitude, finding his way back to me through the convolutions of time, space and eternity.

In this book I have related many things, teachings, that I have learned from Tom and other dogs. The practice of mindful dog teaching encompasses not only our attempts to teach our dogs by developing functional relationships with them. It also holds within it the teachings of the very mindful species known as Dog, a species which has adopted, enraptured and uplifted the spirit of humanity, helping us become more than we ever could be alone.

Thank you.

* *

Eros need not end; in fact, I believe it never does. Though our animals may leave us, they remain in our hearts, minds and spirits, our lives forever changed because of the time they spent with us, and we with them. This is another reason why engagement is so important: to provide a basis upon which we may disengage with the satisfaction of knowing we, with our dog, lived that relationship, with order and balance, to its fullest capacity.

* *

Practicing the Concepts in Chapter 7

1. Release

    This is an invocation which helped me cope with Kiwi's illness. Repeat it as often as needed in challenging situations.

    > I set my intent to release whatever is not in this dog's best or highest good, and to send it to its appointed place in the light. I ask for guidance, and I accept what comes.

2. Grief

   Allow yourself to work through the five stages of grieving for your dog, just as you would for a human. Dogs give us many gifts that humans are incapable of giving. The loss of these unique gifts is real and profound. Dignify that loss through respectful grieving and ceremony for your lost companion, and discount any opinions that grieving for an animal is inappropriate.

3. Acceptance

   This visualization has helped my clients who have lost animal companions, especially under traumatic circumstances. If possible, ask someone to read the words to you while you do the visualizing.

   ❖ Sit comfortably with your eyes closed. Rest your hands on your knees, palms up.

   ❖ See the trauma you experienced with your animal's passing; see it resting in your upturned palms.

   ❖ As you gently cradle this hurt and pain, imagine it becoming surrounded by a bubble of white light.

   ❖ The light is infusing every part of the trauma, shining so brightly that the pain and hurt become invisible. This dazzling, beautiful white light permeates every part of the memory of pain and grief.

   ❖ Cradle this dazzling bubble of light in your hands, feeling it's warmth.

   ❖ As the pain and grief and trauma dissolve into the dazzling light, now imagine your departed animal companion within this bubble.

❖ Imagine the white light becoming a soft, rosy pink, the color of love, surrounding your animal with a soft glow.

❖ Your companion is whole, and perfect, beautiful and special. Your eyes meet and you exchange feelings of safety, love and hopefulness.

❖ Now look into the distance. See an angel approaching. A brilliant, beautiful angel with an aura of golden light.

❖ Imagine this angel reaching out to you, to gently take from you this bubble of pink light which you hold in your hands, and which contains the spirit of your beloved companion.

❖ You lift your hands to the angel, passing the spirit of your animal companion into the light of the next world, as you thank your animal for the joy, learning and other gifts she has brought to you during your time together.

❖ You watch the angel depart, certain that you keep in your heart the precious memories of your time together, and knowing that engagement with this transcended animal spirit is just a thought away.

❖ Open your eyes, take a deep breath, remember and rejoice that "there is no death, but only a change of worlds" – Chief Seattle.

* * * * * * * * * * * * * * * * * * * *

Our ancestors achieved a symbiosis, a mutually beneficial relationship, with the dogs in their environment. My wish for you is that you may achieve this symbiosis with your companion dog, in all its evolved richness. May you and your dog receive all the blessings you need to complete your lifes' paths, and may you feel infinite joy, wonder, love and gratitude in your union.

The world is round and the place that may seem like the end may also be only the beginning

— Anon.

References

Introduction

Andrews, T. (2001). *Animal speak.* St. Paul, MN: Llewellyn Publications.

Bekoff, M. and Allen, C. (1997). *Species of mind: the philosophy and biology of cognitive ethology.* Cambridge, MA: The MIT Press.

Masson, J.M. and McCarthy, S. (1995). *When elephants weep: the emotional lives of animals.* New York: Dell Publishing.

Webster's ninth new collegiate dictionary (1989). Springfield MA: Merriam-Webster, Inc., *Publishers*

Chapter 1

Bekoff, M. (2000). *The smile of a dolphin.* New York: Discovery Books/Random House.

Boone, J.A. (1954). *Kinship with all life.* San Francisco: Harper San Francisco.

Clothier, S. (1996). *Finding a balance.* Stanton, NJ: Flying Dog Press.

Cormier, W.H. and Cormier, L.S. (1991). *Interviewing strategies for helpers.* Pacific Grove, CA: Brooks/Cole Publishing Co.

Grandin, T. and Johnson, C. (2005). *Animals in translation: using the mysteries of autism to decode animal behavior.* New York: Scribner.

Grof, S. (1985). *Beyond the brain.* Albany, NY: State University of New York.

Lewis, S.J. (2006). *Java: the true story of a shelter dog who rescued a woman.* St. Paul, MN: Moon Dog Press.

Mc Auliffe, C.E. (2001). *Lucy won't sit.* Oconomowoc WI: Kindness Canine Behavior Consultants.

Wall, S. and Arden, H. (1990). W*isdomkeepers: meetings with native American spiritual elders.* Hillsboro, OR: Beyond Words Publishing, Inc.

Wingfield, J.C. (2003). *Control of behavioral strategies for capricious environments.* Animal Behaviour, 66: 807-816.

Chapter 2

Abrantes, R, (1997). *Dog language.* Naperville, IL: Wakan Tanka Publishers.

Hauser, M.D. (2000). *The evolution of communication.* Cambridge, MA: The MIT Press.

Levey, J. and Levey, M. (1998). *Living in balance.* Berkeley, CA: Conari Press.

Pongracz, P., Miklosi, A., Kubinyi, E., Topal, J., and Csanyi, V. (2003). *Interaction between individual experience and social learning in dogs.* Animal Behaviour, 65: 595-603.

Rugaas, T. (1997). *On talking terms with dogs.* Kula, HI: Legacy by Mail.

Sheldrake, R. (1999). *Dogs that know when their owners are coming home.* New York: Crown Publishers.

Wingfield, J.C. (2003). *Control of behavioural strategies for capricious environments.* Animal Behaviour, 66: 807-816.

Chapter 3

Clothier, S. (1996). *Finding a balance.* Stanton, NJ: Flying Dog Press.

Coppinger, R. and Coppinger, L. (2001). *Dogs: a startling new understanding of canine origin, behavior & evolution.* New York: Scribner.

De Waal, F. (2001). *The ape and the sushi master.* New York: Basic Books.

Maslow, A.H. (1968). *Toward a psychology of being, 2nd ed.* New York: Van Nostrand Reinhold.

Masson, J.M. and McCarthy, S. (1995). *When elephants weep: the emotional lives of animals.* New York: Dell Publishing.

Mc Auliffe, C.E. (2001). *Lucy won't sit.* Oconomowoc WI: Kindness Canine Behavior Consultants

Morris, D. (1986). *Dogwatching.* New York: Crown Trade Paperbacks.

Napier, R.W. and Gershenfeld, M.K. (1993). *Groups: theory and experience.* Boston: Houghton Mifflin Company.

Tellington-Jones, L. (1993). *The tellington ttouch: a revolutionary natural method to train and care for your favorite animal.* New York: Penguin Putnam, Inc.

Chapter 4

Call, J., Brauer, J., Kaminski, J. and Tomasello, M. (2003). *Domestic dogs (canis familiaris) are sensitive to the attentional state of humans.* Journal of Comparative Psychology, 117(3): 257-263.

Coren, S. (2004). *How dogs think.* New York: Free Press.

Grosjean, N. (1999). *Veterinary aromatherapy.* Saffron Walden, Essex, UK: The CW Daniel Company Limited.

Lindsay, S.R. (2005). *Handbook of applied dog behavior and training, volume 3: procedures and protocols.* Ames IA: Blackwell Publishing Professional.

Mc Auliffe, C.E. and Norby, M. (2004). *The good behavior game.* Oconomowoc, WI: Kindness Canine Behavior Consultants LLC.

McConnell, P.B. (1996). *How to be the leader of the pack.* Black Earth, WI: Dog's Best Friend, Ltd.

McConnell, P.B. (2002). *The other end of the leash.* New York: Ballantine Books.

Pongracz, P., Miklosi, A., et.al. (2001). Social *learning in dogs: the effect of a human demonstrator on the performance of dogs in a detour task.* Animal Behaviour, 62: 1109-1117.

Pongracz, P., Miklosi, A., et.al. (2003). Preference *for copying unambiguous demonstrations in dogs (canis familiaris).* Journal of Comparative Psychology, 117(3): 337-343.

Serpell, J. (1995). *The domestic dog: its evolution, behaviour and interactions with people.* Cambridge, UK: Cambridge University Press.

Tellington-Jones, L. (1993). *The tellington ttouch: a revolutionary natural method to train and care for your favorite animal.* New York: Penguin Putnam, Inc.

Chapter 5

Berger, K.S. (2001). *The developing person through the life span, 5th ed.* New York: Worth Publishers.

Bolton, R. (1979). *People skills.* Englewood Cliffs: Prentice-Hall, Inc.

Clothier, S. (1996). *Finding a balance.* Stanton, NJ: Flying Dog Press.

Kouzes, J.M. and Posner, B.Z. (1993). *Credibility.* San Francisco: Jossey-Bass Publishers.

Maslow, A.H. (1968). *Toward a psychology of being, 2nd ed.* New York: Van Nostrand Reinhold.

Masson, J.M. and McCarthy, S. (1995). *When elephants weep: the emotional lives of animals.* New York: Dell Publishing.

McConnell, P.B. (2001). *Feeling outnumbered?* Black Earth, WI: Dog's Best Friend Ltd.

McConnell, P.B. (1996). *How to be the leader of the pack.* Black Earth, WI: Dog's Best Friend Ltd.

Moore, T. (1994). *Care of the soul.* New York: Harper Collins Publishers.

Scott, J.P. and Fuller, J.L. (1965).*Genetics and the social behavior of the dog.* Chicago, IL: The University of Chicago Press.

Tellington-Jones, L. (2001). *Getting in ttouch with your dog.* North Pomfret, VT: Trafalgar Square Publishing.

Topal, J., Gacsi, M., Miklosi, A., et.al. (2005). Attachment *to humans: a comparative study on hand-reared wolves and differently socialized dog puppies.* Animal Behaviour, 70: 1367-1375.

Wikipedia.org. (2006) EROS. Retrieved August 7, 2006, from http://en.wikipedia.org/wiki/EROS

Chapter 6

Berger, K.S. (2001). *The developing person through the life span, 5th ed.* New York: Worth Publishers.

Blood, D.C. and Studdert, V.P. (1999). *Saunders comprehensive veterinary dictionary, 2nd ed.* New York: W.B. Saunders.

Boone, J.A. (1954). *Kinship with all life.* San Francisco: Harper San Francisco.

Chopra, D. (2003). *The spontaneous fulfillment of desire.* New York: Harmony Books.

Eaton, E.J. (2004). Personal communication.

Emoto, M. (2004). *The hidden messages in water.* Hillsboro, OR: Beyond Words Publishing, Inc.

Gardner, H. (1983). *Frames of mind: theory of multiple intelligences.* New York: Basic.

Grandin, T. and Johnson, C. (2005). *Animals in translation: using the mysteries of autism to decode animal behavior.* New York: Scribner.

Grof, S. (1985). *Beyond the brain.* Albany, NY: State University of New York.

Itten, J. (1970). *The elements of color.* New York: John Wiley & Sons, Inc.

Kuijl, T.J. (1999). *Art, science and transcendence: a comparison between Tolstoy and Plato.* Retrieved August 7, 2006, from http://www.xs4all.nl/~aikikai/plato/

Lewis, S.J. (2006). *Java: the true story of a shelter dog who rescued a woman.* St. Paul, MN: Moon Dog Press.

Lorenz, K.Z. (1952). *King solomon's ring.* New York: Time Incorporated.

McConnell, P.B. (1990). *Acoustic structure and receiver response in domestic dogs, canis familiaris.* Animal Behavior, 39: 897-904.

Moore, T. (1994). *Care of the soul.* New York: Harper Collins Publishers.

Morgan, M. (2004). *Mutant message down under.* New York: HarperCollins Publishers, Inc.

Overall, K.L. (1997). *Clinical behavioral medicine for small animals.* St. Louis, MO: Mosby-Year Book, Inc.

Pert, C. (1997). *Molecules of emotion.* New York: Touchstone.

Rooney, N.J., Bradshaw, J.W.S. and Robinson, I.A. (2001). *Do dogs respond to play signals given by humans?* Animal Behaviour, 61: 715-722.

Rugaas, T. (1997). *On talking terms with dogs.* Kula, HI: Legacy by Mail.

Shafarman, S. (1997). *Awareness heals: the Feldenkrais method for dynamic health.* Reading, MA: Perseus Books.

Sheldrake, R. (1999). *Dogs that know when their owners are coming home.* New York: Crown Publishers.

Sherwin, C. and Glen, E.F. (2003). *Cage colour preferences and effects of home cage colour on anxiety in laboratory mice.* Animal Behaviour, 66: 1085-1092.

Tellington-Jones, L. (2002). *Unleash your dog's potential.* North Pomfret, VT: Trafalgar Square Publishing, Inc.

Tellington-Jones, L. (2005). *From linda's desk.* Staying in TTouch, 9(1): 1-2.

Wilson, S.I. and Edlund, T. (2001). *Neural induction: toward a unifying mechanism.* Nature Neuroscience Supplement, 4: 1161-1168.

Woodhouse, B. (1992). *How your dog thinks.* Letchworth, England: Ringpress.

Chapter 7

Andrews, T. (2001). *Animal speak.* St. Paul, MN: Llewellyn Publications.

De Waal, F. (2001). *The ape and the sushi master.* New York: Basic Books.

Grof, S. (1985). *Beyond the brain.* Albany, NY: State University of New York.

Lincoln, K. with Slagle, A.L. (1987). *The good red road.* New York: Harper & Rowe, Publishers, San Francisco.

Masson, J.M. and McCarthy, S. (1995). *When elephants weep: the emotional lives of animals.* New York: Dell Publishing.

McConnell, P.B. (2002). *The other end of the leash.* New York: Ballantine Books.

Sheldrake, R. (1999). *Dogs that know when their owners are coming home.* New York: Crown Publishers.

Smith, P. (1999). *Animal talk.* Hillsboro: Beyond Words Publishing, Inc.

Thomas, E.M. (1993). *The hidden life of dogs.* New York: Simon & Shuster, Inc.

About the Author

Claudeen E. Mc Auliffe is a teacher, lecturer and author. She holds a Master's degree in Education from the University of Wisconsin-Milwaukee, and is a Level 2 Tellington TTouch™ practitioner. She owns and operates Kindness Canine Behavior Consultants in Oconomowoc WI, a consulting practice providing holistic behavior modification for dogs and Tellington TTouch™ workshops for companion animals. Her published works include *Lucy Won't Sit: How to Use Your Body, Mind and Voice for a Well-Behaved Dog, The Big Bang: How You Can Help Your Dog Cope with Thunderstorms and Fireworks, The Good Behavior Game*, and numerous articles and essays.

She is a member of the Association of Pet Dog Trainers (APDT), the Animal Behavior Society, and the Tellington TTouch™ Practitioners' Guild. She is a doctoral student in holistic nutrition and companion animal health at Clayton College of Natural Health in Birmingham, Alabama.